UGANDA
FIRE & BLOOD

Logos International
Plainfield, New Jersey

BY THE SAME AUTHOR
The Taming of the Tongue
Love One Another
Pedro Menendez de Aviles, and the Founding of St.
    Augustine
The Melbourne Bicentennial Book.

Copyright © 1977 by Logos International
All Rights Reserved
Printed in the United States of America
ISBN: 0-88270-237-8
Library of Congress Catalog Card Number:77-78340
Published by Logos International,
Plainfield, New Jersey 07061

ACKNOWLEDGMENTS

This book could never have been written without the assistance of many people all over the world who provided me with essential material and facts concerning the martyrs.

First of all, I give the greatest of thanks to Sister Marie-Andre du Sacre Coeur, a White Sister. In addition to mailing me out of print books and magazines about the martyrs, she sent me an autographed copy of her own definitive book on the subject, *Uganda, Terre de Martyrs*. But even more generous still, she loaned me the precious documents of her interviews, handwritten in the early part of this century, with eyewitnesses of the holocaust and relatives and descendants of the saints. In addition, she wrote me many letters in answer to my endless questions.

I also extend my gratitude to the Reverend E. I. Demkovich, W. F. and secretary of the Martyrs of Uganda Center in Washington, D.C. He provided me with additional rare material as well as further answers to queries. The White Fathers have been very helpful in providing factual assistance as regards names, spellings and dates, as well as donating the use of their treasured collection of photographs of the period.

My primary source of information on the Anglican martyrs was selected and provided by a lifetime friend, the late Sister Anita, an Episcopal Sister of the Holy Nativity. She mailed me the out of print books published in the late nineteenth century about the work of the English missionaries in Uganda. Fortunately for me, she was the research librarian, until her recent death, at the Margaret Peabody Lending Library, run by the Sisters of the Holy Nativity at their convent in Fond du Lac, Wisconsin.

Other important material, documents as well as news clippings from Kampala were sent me by the Right Reverend Dunstan Nsubuga, Anglican bishop of Namirembe. A copy of the canonization process was sent in from Rome by the Reverend Herman Verhaeghe, procurator general of the White Fathers.

I extend particular thanks to the Right Reverend Leslie Brown, bishop of St. Edmundsbury, England, as well as a former archbishop of Kampala. He airmailed me the obituaries which he wrote for the *London Times* as well as *The Church Times*, containing extensive biographical sketches of his late friend and co-worker in the field, Janani Luwum. Additional personal glimpses were sent me by the Right Reverend Robert C. Rusack, Bishop of the Episcopal Diocese of Los Angeles, California, who attended Canterbury College with Janani Luwum.

Last, but not least, particular thanks to my editor, Dennis Baker.

Elaine Murray Stone
Melbourne, Florida
March, 1977

PROLOGUE

The black archbishop stood in purple vestments before his accuser. Like Jesus, at a similar trial so long ago, he did not plead for mercy, nor attempt to defend himself.

The charge, made by Ugandan President Idi Amin Dada, in front of a crowd of three thousand assembled outside the Nile Gardens Hotel, was that the Most Reverend Janani Luwum, Anglican archbishop of Uganda, Rwanda, Burundi and Boga-Zaire, had plotted to assassinate him and overthrow his regime.

But Archbishop Luwum, who was fifty-three, was not the sort of person one associates with an assassin's role. Born into a traditionally Christian tribe, he was educated at Anglican colleges both in Uganda and Britain. While at Canterbury's Saint Augustine College, he was known as the East African "Ivy

League" churchman, because he wore grey flannel slacks, a Harris Tweed sports jacket and school tie. At the Lambeth Conference of 1968 he was advisor to the bishops on the church in East Africa. In 1969 he was consecrated bishop of Northern Uganda, and following the withdrawal of the English, including Archbishop Leslie Brown, was consecrated the first black archbishop of that area in 1974.

Beloved by fellow students, and later clergy and bishops under his charge, he was known for his humility, devotion, and particularly the winsome smile that charmed everyone who knew him.

But underneath Luwum's charm and urbanity, beat a fearless heart. Aware of the consequences, he constantly reminded Amin of the immorality of his acts—which ultimately brought about his arrest.

Also arrested with the archbishop were two cabinet members, Charles Oboth-Ofumbi, Ugandan minister for internal affairs, and Erinayo Oryema, minister of land and water resources.

The three stood helpless before the menacing crowd which, stirred by Amin's military henchmen, shouted accusations. When the charges were read, the archbishop was seen to shake his head in unbelief. Angered, Amin thundered at him, "You did it. I know. God himself told me so!"

Like most despots, Amin is in constant fear for his life. Over the past few years he has been the target of eleven attempted assassinations. And no wonder. Since he seized power in 1971 from his predecessor, Milton Obote, Uganda has fallen from being one of the most modernized nations of East Africa to become a chamber of blood and horror racing toward economic ruin.

A fourth grade dropout, the 240-pound tyrant

reigns with a fist of iron, torturing and murdering all who stand in his way. Amin is a Moslem from near the Sudan. He hates Christian, Jew and Hindu alike and has instigated pogroms against all except fellow Moslems who comprise but five percent of the population of Uganda.

For many decades Christians have been the ruling class in this country, members of the former royal court having embraced the faith long ago. Both Catholics and Anglicans have held top posts in government and education. Amin considers all of them a threat to his rule.

President Nyerere of neighboring Tanzania harbors Amin's predecessor, Obote, an Anglican, and calls Amin's "one of the most murderous administrations in all Africa." Relations with Kenya are no better, as Amin has not hesitated to massacre Kenyans living in Uganda. Escaping Kenyans are, in fact, a chief source of news about atrocities in Uganda.

There are nearly seven million Christians in the nation. With so many followers, the bishops could attain greater power than Amin himself, or so he reasons. Consequently, if bishops in any way stand up to the Moslem despot, he removes them by expulsion or death. Archbishop Luwum, leader of the eighteen Anglican bishops under his jurisdiction, made a prime target.

Inflamed by the oratory of their uniformed president, who played on their sympathy by announcing that he had almost died in an assassination attempt, the troops shouted "Kill them! Kill them today!"

The archbishop and two government ministers were roughly shoved into a Land Rover, presumably to be driven to the military prison outside of Kampala for trial. The three were never seen alive again.

News of their arrest and public humiliation made headlines all over the world. The next day, on Thursday, February 17th, 1977, word came via official government sources that one of the ministers had attempted to overpower the driver of the Land Rover. In the ensuing accident, the archbishop and both cabinet ministers had been killed. The driver, severely injured, was taken to a hospital in Kampala.

Days later, the archbishop's body was buried hurriedly with neither clergy nor members of his family present. The interment was at Kitgum, Luwum's birthplace, over seventy miles from the capital. But everything about the accident and burial seemed strange and suspicious. Rumors began to leak out through neighboring Tanzania and Kenya.

The rumors asserted that, among other things, the body of the archbishop had three bullet holes in it—two in the chest, and one in the mouth. The bodies of all three victims had been dumped into Lake Victoria. Then, on Monday, February 21st, the government-owned Tanzanian newspaper, the *Daily News*, printed the bizarre story that President Amin had personally shot the Anglican archbishop.

The dispatch stated that following his arrest, Luwum had been taken to a private lodge for a meeting wth Amin. After repeatedly refusing to sign a prepared confession stating he had plotted to topple Amin, the archbishop was stripped and made to lie on the floor.

"Two soldiers in turn whipped the archbishop. And while they did so, the archbishop uttered prayers. But the prayers seemed to have incensed Amin, for he angrily shouted wildly in extremely obscene language and struck the archbishop. . . ."

The news story continued, "Shortly before 8 A.M. there were very bizarre, sacrilegious and obscene activities, during which Amin pulled out his pistol and shot the archbishop twice on the left side of the chest." Luwum died instantly and in the morning his body along with the bodies of the two murdered cabinet ministers were dumped into the lake.

As soon as this tale of martyrdom and savagery reached the civilized world, Amin backed up his version of the auto accident first with a photo of the death car, then with staged TV coverage of an interview with the car's chauffeur, Major Moses, outside the hospital where he was recuperating.

But all through that eventful week, February 14th-22nd, 1977, news of frightful pogroms against Christians squeaked through the tight curtain of security around Amin's African dictatorship. Bodies were seen clogging the waterways and dams of the Nile. According to the *Los Angeles Times,* one thousand Ugandans were killed and hundreds more arrested and tortured in a two-week reign of terror. Women and children were reported machine-gunned in revenge for the alleged revolutionary plot.

Amin contends that the Christian soldiers of the Acholi and Langi tribes were gathering to attack and overthrow his administration. Both of these tribes have been Catholic for almost one hundred years. There had always existed tension between them and the Moslem tribes. Amin ordered two thousand of these Christian soldiers transported to Mubende and Kbamba where they were mutilated and shot.

Next he zeroed in on the campuses, centers of higher education originally founded by Anglican churchmen. Soldiers swarmed over Kampala's famed Makerere University, arresting Christian students and professors, killing some publicly, others in isolated prisons. Screams from those being tortured were heard all week by people in the vicinity of the capital's prisons.

And what better way to scatter the flock than by destroying their shepherds. In addition to the murder of the archbishop, a native Ugandan, Amin ordered more than one hundred Christian missionaries to leave Uganda. He continues to defend his actions and atrocities by saying he has received his instructions from God, "Uganda must be a Moslem country."

The Right Reverend Leslie Brown, Luwum's predecessor as archbishop in Kampala, now bishop of St. Edmundsbury in England, said, on his return from memorial services for Luwum in Nairobi, Kenya, "I was told by an eyewitness that the archbishop had been shot to death. The archbishop had a bullet hole on each side of his chest, and was also shot in the mouth."

The Archbishop of Canterbury, Dr. Donald Coggan, said in an interview, "I never was in doubt that the archbishop of Uganda was murdered. This is just a flare-up of months of incidents." He added that Amin should be barred from attending Queen Elizabeth's silver jubilee celebration this June in Britain.

In spite of the accumulation of this sordid evidence, Amin continues to protest his innocence and maintains that the three men died in an auto accident. He invited international newsmen to view the scene of the accident and film TV footage of the area, the car and the driver. However, he refused to allow anyone to view the bodies.

Amin has reportedly imagined a plot by the American, British and Israeli governments to invade his country with parachute troops. He was apparently indignant at President Carter's remarks about Amin's "disgusting" behavior and began to harass and intimidate American residents in Uganda, mostly missionaries and a few airline employees (the United States maintains no embassy in Uganda). A spokesman for Amin insisted there was no cause for alarm, but Amin is an alarming person. His first wife was almost killed in a staged auto accident, while his second wife was found dismembered in the trunk of an auto.

None of this violence and horror is new to Uganda, as this book will amply demonstrate. Idi Amin Dada stands firmly in the tradition of his forebears—a tradition of torture and bloodshed. It is as if the nation stands under a curse.

But, until the airport at Entebbe became the site of a rescue by Israeli commandos that gained the attention of the entire world, Uganda stood with its curse in relative obscurity. Now, with the gruesome execution of one of Africa's leading churchmen, what Idi Amin has been doing in relative secrecy is being proclaimed from the rooftops.

Once one of the most commercially prosperous countries of Africa, Uganda is being strangled by Amin's mindlessly militaristic policies which seem governed and shaped most of all by Amin's paranoiac cruelty. For example, just a few years ago he expelled the Asians who lived in Uganda under British passports. They constituted the mercantile backbone of the country, but, because Amin hated them as predominantly Hindu foreigners, they were driven out. But his greatest atrocities have been inflicted on native Ugandans. Since he took power from Milton Obote in 1971, nearly three hundred thousand people have disappeared. Most, if not all of them, have undoubtedly suffered violent deaths. News and feature stories often recount grim reports of the crocodiles of the Nile and Lake Victoria growing fat on human carcasses.

Most of the Ugandans being killed by Amin are, like Archbishop Luwum, Christians. They comprise about sixty percent of the 11-million-plus population. And they possess a heritage of martyrdom. The news of Luwum's murder reached the rest of the world in less than a day, but, in 1886, similar news took months to reach Europe. Carried by runners and by boat through jungles and across immense Lake Victoria to the East African coast and thence by steamer to England and Italy, it told of scores of brave young Christians who gave their lives rather than deny Christ. Their sacrifice effectively changed the course of Ugandan history.

Who were these martyrs? How had they become converted to Christianity? Why did they die? What has been their impact upon Africa and, indeed, Western culture? To answer these questions we'll go back to the first European explorations north and west of Lake Victoria in the mid-nineteenth century. And the answers we find will help to make sense of what is happening today in that unhappy country.

Table of Contents

CHAPTER ONE

CHRISTIANITY
COMES TO UGANDA

Today you can reach central Africa within hours by plane from almost any great city in the world. But only a century ago this interior heartland of the largest land mass of the southern hemisphere was virtually unknown to most of the rest of the world. When Europeans spoke of "The Dark Continent" in the nineteenth century the phrase had special reference to the center of the continent, for the coastlands of the Mediterranean, the Atlantic and the Indian Oceans were all well known to them. North Africa was the haunt of Europeans even in antiquity. South Africa, by the nineteenth century, was already well populated with Englishmen, Germans and Dutchmen. And commerce in slaves, ivory, coffee and numerous other goods made European sailors quite familiar with the other coastlands.

But owing to the impenetrable jungles, high

mountains, impassable swamps, and vast deserts, central Africa still remained a mystery, unexplored and free of European conquest.

Uganda, situated on the northwestern shore of the immense inland body of water, later named Lake Victoria, was at that time still unvisited by a European. Arabs had penetrated from the north, up the Nile, around the lake, bringing with them the slave trade, cotton cloth, and the Moslem faith. They also introduced smoking, firearms, and homosexuality.

But by the mid-1860s, several English explorers happened upon Uganda at almost the same time. They were J.H. Speke and J.A. Grant who, traveling around the western shore of Lake Victoria, arrived at the Bugandan* capital in 1862. The tribal king, Mutesa, not happy about the arrival of the white foreigners, tried to discourage the explorers from continuing their journey. Mutesa was also worried about news of slavers penetrating into his country from the Sudan just to the north, and desired to keep all foreigners out of his country, whether white or black.

However, both Speke and Grant, through the means of many gifts, were able to persuade the king to permit them to continue their journey, in which they ultimately discovered the source of the White Nile near Jinja in July, 1862. Enduring the most severe hardships, they followed the uncharted rivers through the Sudan and into Egypt, proving undeniably their theory of its source.

Another explorer, the wealthy Sir Samuel Baker,

---

* Buganda was the southernmost and most powerful of the four tribal kingdoms that comprise modern-day Uganda. The terms Uganda and Baganda are used, in this book, somewhat interchangeably. The term Baganda refers to the tribesmen of the entire vicinity, regardless of their specific tribal affiliation. Two other words in the native tongue of Luganda occur frequently in this book, *Kabaka*, which means king, and *Katakiro*, which means chancellor.

accompanied by his wife, received pertinent information from Speke and Grant when they met by accident at Gondokoro, went on to discover Lake Albert in 1864.

Then in 1869, Uganda received a genuine threat to its isolation and unchallenged monarchy, when the forces of the Khedive Ishmail of Egypt penetrated its borders. This ruler of Egypt was very ambitious and wished to expand his holdings to the countries south of him.

He employed the famous English soldier, Colonel Charles George Gordon, to head his native forces, and in 1870, Gordon, carrying the Egyptian flag, swept into Uganda. He was restrained from building a chain of forts only through King Mutesa's adroit diplomacy. Mutesa saw nothing in this move to control slavery, but an underhanded bid to take over his country and his throne.

The missionary period began in Uganda when the journalist-explorer, Sir Henry Morton Stanley, arrived there in 1875.

Stanley was born John Rowlands in Wales in 1841. Orphaned at an early age, he was tossed from one relative to another, from school to workhouse, until at the age of sixteen, he sailed to New Orleans as a cabin boy. There he was adopted by wealthy newspaper owner, Henry Morton Stanley, who also gave him his name.

When the Civil War broke out, Stanley enlisted in the Confederate Army. Following his capture at Shiloh, he fought with the federal artillery forces. Still later, he enlisted in the United States Navy.

After this varied experience during the war, he took off for Salt Lake City where he began his career as a journalist. His reports as a correspondent for the

Missouri Democrat, while with General Hancock's expedition against the Indians, led to his receiving a commission from the *New York Herald* to accompany the British forces in their 1867 expedition against Emperor Theodosius of Abyssinia. His outstanding news sense and courageous travels to many obscure places of the world eventually led to Stanley becoming the leading journalist of his day.

In 1869, the top news was the story of the missing missionary, David Livingstone, who had gone to central Africa and had not been heard from since. Convinced that Livingstone was still alive, the owner of the *New York Herald*, James Gordon Bennett, commissioned Stanley to go to Africa in search of him.

Arriving in Zanzibar in January, 1871, Stanley trekked west at the head of a huge caravan of porters from March until November 10th, when he discovered the illusive missionary outside a grass hut in Ujiji. It was then that Stanley greeted him, "Dr. Livingstone, I presume."

After doing some exploring on the northern shores of Tanganyika, and settling questions of hydrography of the Nile basin, Stanley returned to England to receive the plaudits of the world.

Stanley's book, *How I Found Livingstone*, became a runaway best seller, and to those who doubted that he had really discovered the missionary, he revealed the personal journals of Livingstone which he had brought back with him as proof.

Next followed a series of lectures all over England and the United States, increasing his fame and fortune. Hearing of the tragic death of Livingstone in 1874, and desiring to return to Africa for further explorations, Stanley looked about for the money he would need. A fund was raised by Lord Burnham and

Gordon Bennett, Jr., for an Anglo-American Expedition to be led by Stanley and to depart for Africa in October, 1874.

The three-year expedition resulted in Stanley discovering the course of the Congo River, the length and size of Lake Victoria—which turned out to be two hundred miles long—and, best of all, a navigable waterway penetrating to the heart of Africa.

In 1875, Stanley reached Uganda. Ushered into the impressive audience hall of King Mutesa, he described to the very interested African monarch the wonders of civilization and the benefits of Christianity.

Mutesa was hemmed in on several borders by militant Moslems who continually threatened his domain. Learning of the tremendous strength and power of the Christian nations, such as England and the United States, he called together his chiefs and urged upon them the need to accept Christianity when it should be available to them. He was intimidated by Egypt and the Islamic powers, and hoped that embracing the Christian faith would bring with it the protection of the great Christian nations about which the talented journalist had painted an impressive picture.

Stanley was detained at the Bugandan court for several weeks because of a battle being fought with Mutesa's enemies on Buvuma Island. He made use of this period to teach the absolute monarch the Lord's Prayer, the Ten Commandments, and the Golden Rule. He also prevailed upon Mutesa to require the court to observe the Christian sabbath in addition to the Moslem one which they had already adopted.

Continuing his travels, he first sent an historic letter to his two newspapers, the *London Daily Telegraph* and the *New York Tribune*, concerning the needs of the

Africans, which was carried back to civilization by Colonel Gordon. The letter was delivered by Linant de Bellefonds, a Frenchman in the service of Gordon, who had arrived at the court of Mutesa shortly after Stanley.

Taking six months to travel from Africa to England, the letter was published on November 15th, 1875, in the *London Daily Telegraph*, carrying Stanley's poignant appeal to the Christian world for missionaries to come to Uganda.

"Oh, that some pious, practical missionary would come here!" wrote the journalist. "What a field-and-harvest ripe for the sickle of civilization! Mutesa would give him anything he desired: houses, land, cattle, ivory, etc. He might call a province his own one day. It is not the mere preacher, however, that is wanted here. It is the practical tutor who can teach the people how to become Christians, cure their diseases, construct dwellings, understand and exemplify agriculture—this is the man that is wanted."

Only eight days after this appeal appeared in print, several thousand pounds had been given for this cause! People were thrilled at the thought of participating in sending the Christian gospel to this recently discovered nation in the center of Africa.

The Church Missionary Society, having decided to undertake the Uganda mission, and already supplied with the funds to make it possible, now turned to those who offered themselves for this dangerous task.

They appointed as head of the mission, Alexander Mackay, a young Scottish engineer. This young bachelor had deep brown eyes, brown hair, and was of shorter than average stature. Not an ordained minister, he had however been educated at the Edinburgh Free Church Teacher Training Institute for which he was eligible, being the son of an impecunious Presbyterian minister. Following his matriculation, he journeyed to Germany where he hoped to receive the very best "on-the-job training" available in highly advanced fields.

Feeling a distinct call to missionary work, he offered his services to the Church Missionary Society. Shortly after that, Mackay, at the age of twenty-seven, found himself in Madagascar, working as an engineering missionary.

Finding the island people not sufficiently advanced to make proper use of his engineering training, he asked to be reassigned. Already close to the East African coast, Mackay became the logical choice of the Church Missionary Society to head up the new delegation to Uganda.

A well-equipped party of eight sailed from England to Zanzibar in 1878 under the leadership of Lieutenant Shergold-Smith, with the Reverend C.T. Wilson as the only ordained minister in the group. There they spent the first few months on the African coast hiring porters and making arrangements for the inland trek. During this period, Mackay made use of his engineering talents by assisting the natives in building a road. Unfortunately, this resulted in keeping him from making the long-awaited journey to Uganda because he was severely injured when a wagon fell on him and crushed his leg. The accident detained him on the coast for a year.

The remainder of the party decided to go on ahead without him. After terrible hardships, the only two survivors of the original mission party, the Reverend C.T. Wilson and Lieutenant Shergold-Smith, arrived at last at the court of Mutesa on January 30th, 1877. Shergold-Smith, a short time later, returned to Kagei at the south end of the immense inland lake where he had left a member of their party, Mr. O'Neill, in charge of the heavier baggage, and to complete repairs on a *dhow* which they had purchased for travel on the lake.

The two men packed all the supplies on board the mission boat and set sail for the royal port at Munyonyo. Contrary winds, however, obliged them to put back to Ukerere, where there was an older mission station. Here they became embroiled in a contention between two native rulers. In protecting an Arab named Songoro, both were killed by one of the kings, Lukongeh, in an argument over the true ownership of the *dhow*.

Meanwhile, Mr. Wilson occupied the neat little hut built for them by Mutesa's people on two acres of land in Rubaga, opposite the palace. Located on a hill, it was built of tiger grass, with a high roof thatched with grass and supported by a number of poles. The partitions and doors of the rooms were also made of tiger grass.

He initiated worship services at the palace every Sunday, for which day Mutesa showed a certain respect. The king also began to learn the English alphabet and desired that his people should learn to read and write. He and the rest of his court showed a remarkable readiness to receive religious instruction.

Mr. Wilson, now alone at the court, following the news of the murders of Shergold-Smith and O'Neill at Speke's Gulf, as it was later named, traveled part way back to find Mackay. He was, after a year on the coast, finally making his way overland to the mission station at Kagei, south of Lake Victoria. After a joyous reunion, the two missionaries returned together to the palace at Rubaga where they began their work in earnest.

The ruler of this absolute monarchy, *Kabaka* (meaning King) Mutesa, had been ailing and in bad spirits. But Mackay enthralled him with his mechanical talents and pleased him with his knowledge of Swahili learned during his year of recuperation from the accident.

Soon his efforts paid off. The king allowed the mission to conduct church services at court, and initiate Bible reading classes. Very soon, Christianity superseded Islam at the palace. Mutesa said to one of the Arabs at court, "Today, I have heard the truth. There can be only one truth, Your religion is different from the truth—therefore it must be false."

A few months later, Mackay was able to write, "The king and I are great friends and his chiefs also have confidence in me."

After four months, the first two missionaries were joined by three others who had come by way of the Nile. They were the Reverend G. Litchfield, the Reverend C.W. Pearson and the Reverend R.W. Felkin, all priests of the Church of England. These new missionaries had come up the Nile, through the Sudan, with the help of Colonel Charles Gordon. Gordon's forces were situated on the northern border of Uganda. The king did not like to have foreign troops so close at hand. He made this quite clear to the Anglican missionaries, who tried to assure the king that their fellow Englishmen had no intentions of invading his kingdom, but were just there for the protection of the British in the Sudan.

Mutesa was a wily king, and decided that if the English missionaries could control the actions of this famed warrior and prevent him from molesting or invading his country, then it was best to have them on his side. He listened intently to their preaching and

9

required the chiefs to observe the Christian sabbath and memorize the Lord's Prayer which Mackay had now finally translated into their mother tongue of Luganda.

However, Mutesa fluctuated hesitantly from his old pagan beliefs, to Islam and Christianity and back again. When in 1879 he became quite ill, Mutesa called in the mediums of his tribal gods to cure him of the disease. Mackay was very disturbed. He had felt the king was about to become a Christian, and therefore tried to prevent the sorcerers from treating him. Mutesa was furious. Relations at the court became seriously strained. Mackay informed the king that the English missionaries were even considering leaving the country because of his disloyalty.

Mutesa, hearing this, had a change of heart. The displeasure of the English could mean the loss of their friendship and protection from an invasion by the Moslem Egyptians.

The five English missionaries then began building their mission house a few miles from the royal enclosure. Shortly after their arrival, they had printed copies of two Gospels in Luganda on a small portable press, in addition to the complete New Testament in Swahili. They now invited the members of the court, numbering several thousand, to come to the mission for instruction in reading and writing conducted primarily with excerpts from the Bible.

In conjunction with the reading classes, they began lessons in the Church of England cathechism, which had also been translated into the native languages. Four catechumens were baptized by the Reverend Mr. O'Flaherty in March, 1879, and the mission had many others under instruction.

The Buganda seemed to be a more than ordinary

intelligence and strength of character. They learned quickly and applied most devoutly the lessons in Christian living which the missionaries taught them.

Among the earliest group of those studying at the Anglican mission was Joseph Mukasa, who later joined the Roman Catholics and became the first of the Catholic Ugandan martyrs to sacrifice his life for Christ.

The work of the missionaries was slow, and not many conversions took place during the first year. However, it was the rule amongst most denominations in Africa to require a study period of several years before admitting the candidate to baptism. This had several purposes. One, it diminished the possibility of backsliding if the life of a Christian should prove too difficult. Two, it gave the neophyte a long postulancy in which he could become truly assured of his belief in God. It was a land of violence and the missionaries knew it would take time for the gospel to seriously penetrate the hearts of its people.

The king of Uganda held absolute power over all his subjects, even the very highly placed chieftains. Executions, torture and maimings took place regularly at the whim of the monarch, or according to the pagan practices of the court. For instance, it was the custom to sacrifice hundreds of tribesmen on the death of a king.

In April of 1880, on the advice of his pagan witch doctors, the king ordered the arrest of all those found wearing their bark cloth togas in a particular way. This was done to collect the required number of victims for sacrifice at the inauguration of the ornamental hut to be placed over the grave of the late king, Suna. Always in multiples of nine, the witch doctors demanded ninety men to be sacrificed at this dedication. The victims, wishing to satisfy the king and bring him the good luck associated with the erecting of the new mausoleum, accepted their fate without protest.

The court of *Kabaka* Mutesa was located on the shores of Lake Victoria at Rubaga and contained over three thousand members. The royal enclosure covered nearly a square mile at the crest of a hill and was completely surrounded by a fence of vertical untrimmed reeds. The largest part was always reserved for the *Kabaka* and his women, which numbered as many as eighty-four wives and a thousand concubines. This area contained almost six hundred buildings constructed of reeds and roofed with tiger grass.

The public part, located to the right of the main gateway, comprised about a quarter of the palace enclosure and was divided by fences into a series of successive courtyards. Here was located the prayer house, which served for pagan, Christian, or Moslem rites, depending on the whim of the *Kabaka* at the moment. Next came a large area, the court of stores in which were kept the plantains and yams, staples of the Ugandan diet, as well as the bark or cotton togas, and later, guns and ammunition. This was followed by a tremendous audience hall in which were situated hundreds of young pages who did much of the work and message-carrying required by such a large and highly organized palace.

Beyond this area was a smaller audience hall in which the *Kabaka* held court seated on an ivory throne, his feet resting on two tremendous, crossed elephant tusks. An oriental rug was placed directly before him while the rest of the hall was strewn with dry grass. He was dressed in a black turkish tunic, white trousers bound in red, and red shoes with a red cap on his head. All subjects approaching Mutesa, the *Kabaka*, had to prostrate themselves before him and could only speak when given permission by the royal chancellor. Replying correctly, following the rapidly changing whims of Mutesa, could be a serious matter of life or death.

Mutesa was in power in a monarchy of three million persons in 1857 when the Arabs came frequently to his court. They attempted to convert the young monarch, but he never officially accepted the Mohammedan religion as it required circumcision as an initiatory rite, although he permitted members of his court to embrace that faith.

Mutesa was very tall and dignified with a Roman nose, long graceful neck and beautiful eyes. He was very much loved by his subjects and made quite an impression on the English when they arrived at his magnificent court. However, the Reverend Robert P. Ashe, one of the later Anglican missionaries to arrive in Uganda, said of him, "There was much that was good and lovable in him, but his education had been a training in cruelty, brutality and lust."

Although Mutesa had over a thousand women to please him, he also sustained unnatural cravings for the young page boys. These were sons of chiefs sent from all over Uganda for their political training at court. Many of them were in their early teens with soft, smooth skin, and laughing, girlish voices.

No sooner had the Anglican priests arrived at the royal enclosure and begun their Christian instruction when they discovered the moral decadence of the monarch and his court. As many of the first converts were among the young pages, it was incumbent upon the clergymen to insist that the boys remain pure from any type of carnal knowledge if they were to receive baptism.

13

This lead to great resentment against the missionaries on the part of the frustrated Mutesa. It also placed the page boy catechumens in great danger of his anger, which at this court could mean instant, or agonizingly prolonged death.

But in spite of the dangers which the Anglican rules and restrictions brought to members of the court, more and more young men showed up regularly at the mission for instruction. Gradually the black colony of baptized members of the Church of England, here in the very heart of Africa, increased. Two workshops were added to the mission, one for the printing press, the other for building carts, furniture and making repairs.

The immensity of the palace enclosure made it possible for the boys to meet together in various smaller courts and huts for regular prayers or classes in reading or catechism. They could go undetected and unafraid, for in such a large community not everyone could know what all the others might be up to.

Mutesa knew there were already nearly one hundred Christians at his court. He often sent for Mr. Mackay or the Reverend Mr. O'Flaherty to give him instruction in the Christian faith, or just in reading, or to tell him about the great white world across the sea.

Then in 1879, something happened which bewildered King Mutesa. A group of Roman Catholic priests arrived at the court and told him of their faith. It was seemingly quite different from that of the Anglican missionaries. Earlier, Mutesa had been torn between the teachings of the Moslem Arabs and the English Christians. Now, of these three, which one was the true religion? The Moslem, the Anglican or this new one—Roman Catholic?

Actually, Mutesa had no serious problem, for he had no intention of abandoning his pagan ways. He was prepared to change his faith, for political reasons only, to whichever one had the most to offer him and his country. Religion had been an instrument of politics in his own kingdom for so long that he was unable to distinguish between the two. He might become a Moslem because the Arabs had supplied him with arms in the past and because it might prevent a takeover by Egypt. But, likewise, it might be helpful to become an Anglican and have behind him the might and power of the tremendous far-flung British Empire. Then again, he could gain much from an alliance with the French Catholics who had just come to the court, as the French were well entrenched in many parts of Africa and could come to his aid. Also, the priests had brought him guns, ornate uniforms and gunpowder.

If acceptance of one of these religions was a condition of military assistance, then he was ready to give *that* religion nominal allegiance. But, just nominal. His heart was still truly devoted to the animistic national pagan practices of his forefathers.

It was in such an environment that the newly arrived French priests found themselves, and they wondered, "Could they succeed in bringing Christ to such a hotbed of corruption?"

CHAPTER TWO

THE CATHOLICS
COME TO UGANDA

The Society of Missionaries of Africa, commonly called the White Fathers because of the white habit and hood which they wear, came into being in 1868. It was the brainchild of Charles Lavigerie, and was started by him in Algeria when he was sent there as Roman Catholic archbishop.

Charles Lavigerie was born in Huile, France, October 31st, 1825. He was an excellent student while at the seminary of Saint Sulpice and was ordained to the priesthood after further studies at Carmel. Because of his aptitude for languages, he was chosen to direct Catholic studies in the Near East, but returned to France when appointed bishop of Nancy.

Nonetheless, his true interest lay in strange and distant lands. He was, therefore, overjoyed when he was sent to Algiers as archbishop. His happiness was soon turned to concern and heartbreak, though, when he saw the frightful conditions in which his North African fellow beings lived.

Famine, cholera and plague struck Algiers in repeated blows, leaving his diocese a charnel house. Everywhere in the squalid streets roamed sickly, starving Arab children, orphaned and homeless. Their plight touched the archbishop's tender heart, and with the assistance of a few French seminarians and priests drawn there by his touching letters, he founded the order now known all over Africa as the White Fathers.

The fathers' first endeavors were with the orphans of Algiers, but the needs of other Africans soon drew them to new territories. They set up mission stations in the Kabylia mountains and along the fringes of the Sahara, bringing food and medicine and the knowledge of Christ to the desert peoples of Africa.

By 1876, Lavigerie decided, in view of the unexpected expansion of his order, that it was time to move across the desert and set up missions to the south. However, the fierce Taureg tribesmen who inhabited the area murdered the devoted fathers as fast as they arrrived.

The archbishop then heard of the recently explored kingdom of Uganda. He decided to by-pass the Tauregs for a period and send his priests into Uganda. He set up a master plan for all the White Fathers, regardless of location.

After establishing themselves in a centrally located spot, they were to gather together orphans and slaves and work among them. Imperative for success was the cultivation of friendship of the local tribal leaders. The converts were to be instructed over a period of four years in a "catechumenate" modeled after that of the early Christian church. It was designed to test the sincerity and fidelity of future converts, the method still used today by the White Fathers.

Of great importance was the training of catechists, chosen from the most dedicated natives, who could carry on the missionary work in outlying areas or when it became necessary for the fathers to leave an area. As it transpired, this very problem arose soon after the White Fathers arrived in Uganda, and their work was carried along for three years by the catechists.

So it was that in 1878, five White Fathers sailed by steamer for Zanzibar, then set out on a westward trek overland for eight hundred miles to Lake Victoria, a six months journey of much hardship. One man was chosen to cross the lake to Entebbe and ask the *Kabaka* for permission to enter his country. This priest was the famous Pere* Simeon Lourdel, the central character in the story of the Uganda martyrs.

Simeon Lourdel was a native of France from the small village of Pas-de-Calais. In his early twenties he joined the Missionary Order of White Fathers and prepared for a lifetime in Africa by zealous study of Swahili.

When he arrived at Mutesa's court, February 23rd, 1879, he was only twenty-six years old, tall, blond with blue eyes, and unusually handsome.

He possessed all the qualities of a leader, and made the first and foremost contact with the king and court, who were astounded at his facility in Swahili, the lingua franca of East Africa.

Beloved by his native Christians, he was the undisputed founder of Catholicism in Uganda.

The *Kabaka*, although disturbed by the arrival of more Europeans at his court, had received a favorable report on the French priests. One of his courtiers, Zoli,

---

* *Pere* is French for "Father," not a proper name.

19

had accompanied the sultan of Madagascar to France in 1875, and assured Mutesa that the French were very good people.

Accordingly, the newcomers were assigned quarters at Kitebbe between Rubaga and the lake. King Mutesa sent a retinue of twenty-four canoes of his own men to bring the other three White Fathers from the south back to his court. These were the French priests, Livinhac, Girault and Barbot.

On their arrival, they were granted an audience at the court. Zoli became their champion and prevailed upon the king to permit them to remain. He even got Mutesa to assign a number of Ugandans plus materials to build a house and chapel for the five White Fathers. This greatly aided the priests in their missionary work. Their first catechumens came from among the natives working on the mission buildings who were impressed by the kindness, gentleness and piety of these men of God.

The first house was completed in September, 1879, and the chapel was ready for a High Mass to be celebrated December 8th, on the Feast of the Immaculate Conception. Catechism classes were started with several of the court pages attending. Vestments and altar vessels had been brought from France.

Father Lourdel was touched by the earnestness of the neophytes and their attendance to their religious duties, so the fathers felt justified in baptizing four of them in March, 1880, and four others in May of that same year. Unfortunately, two of these young men had previously attended reading and catechism classes at the English mission. This added to the hard feelings between the two missionary groups, already having difficulties in maintaining pleasant relationships in this distant land.

In addition to this problem was the vacillation of the king. In July and August, Mutesa had been zealously attending Father Lourdel's catechism classes. Then in September, he informed Mackay that he wished to be baptized in the religion of the Englishmen. Then in October, he asked Father Lourdel to baptize him, and in November he showed signs of returning to Islam. But his deception was unmasked when he sought out the animistic mediums during his illness.

The Catholic fathers thereafter decided to channel all their efforts toward conversion of the people. In May, 1880, a new building was completed for the thirty orphans whom they had taken under their care. Work had also progressed among the many slaves employed about the royal enclosure, when they had the good fortune to number among their converts several men of prominence as well. One of these was Joseph Mukasa, a page in the private apartments of the king, another was Andrew Kaggwa, master-drummer and chief bandmaster of the court, and Mathias Kalemba, head of an important chief's household.

Not content to have the pearl of great price for themselves, these new Catholics imparted the fire of their conversion to all those who worked with them.

As bandmaster, Andrew Kaggwa had under his baton fifteen brightly uniformed drummers, five cymbal players, and ten buglers who were required to play on all festive occasions at the court and especially at receptions for distinguished visitors. Being in such close contact with the court instrumentalists, Andrew most naturally took many of them aside to instruct them in his new found faith. They, in turn, ultimately turned up at the door of the reed mission chapel asking to be received into the church.

Joseph Mukasa was even more advantageously

situated for spreading the faith. Arriving at court at the age of sixteen to serve as a page, he gradually rose in prominence until he became the king's personal attendant. Tall and powerfully built, Mukasa was entrusted with nursing the ailing and cantankerous king. Residing in the innermost sanctum of the court, he was able to influence and inspire many men of rank to enter the folds of the church. Also, his gentleness and patience were an inspiration to the many young pages who went to the Catholic missionaries asking for instruction in how to become good like the kindly Joseph.

Mathias Kalemba began life as a slave when he was carried off from his native Busoga by a raiding party from Uganda. Sold off to a member of the chancellor's family, he was treated more like a son than a servant. He displayed such loyalty and trustworthiness, that he became head of the chief's household, which post he was given officially, with the title of *Mulumba*, on the death of his master.

Tall, light-skinned and pock-marked, Mathias also sported a small beard, most unusual among these tribes. Since his youth he had been looking for the truth, and had tried the faith of the Arabs and then that of the English. But when assigned to oversee the building of the reed house and chapel of the White Fathers, he suddenly realized that he had at last found a faith for which he could gladly lay down his life. However, as a first step toward enrollment as a catechumen he was told he could have only one wife. With great grief he sent away all of his women but one.

After his conversion, Mathias wrote, "God gave me the grace to understand that you taught the truth, and that you really were the men of God about which my father had spoken. Since then I have never had the slightest doubt about the truth of your religion, and I feel truly happy."

Luke Banabakintu was enrolled as a catechumen at the same time as Mathias in May, 1880. He also had received some instruction from the English mission, but neither had been baptized there. At the age of sixteen he entered the service of a chief. Eventually he was appointed supervisor of the cooks, porters, and cutters of wood. He came from a family which had always made canoes for the royal fleet on Lake Victoria. He had a dark, round face and deep, resonant voice, and was of medium height.

Mathias, Luke, Andrew and Joseph were all baptized together on the Feast of Pentecost, 1882, then confirmed by Father Livinhac.* Together these devoted Christians made their first communions at a High Mass.

Before admitting Mathias to the sacraments, Father Livinhac had asked him if he were resolved to persevere. The new Christian replied, his voice trembling with conviction, "Have no fear, Father, it is two years now since I made up my mind, and nothing can change it. I am a Catholic, and I shall die a Catholic." No truer words were ever spoken, although no one then could have dreamed how grimly they would be fulfilled.

All four of these men began to work assiduously to acquire the Christian virtues about which they had learned from the priests. Although each had a position of importance, they now lived simply, humbly and quietly, performing acts of penance and fasting, and earning their keep by the labor of their own hands, something unknown in Uganda for men of their

---

* Livinhac had permission from his immediate superior to do so, as is even now the case where a bishop is impeded from administering confirmation himself.

positions.

Both Mathias and Luke Banabakintu resided about twelve hours walk from the capital, and in their district they soon gathered about themselves a group of catechumens for regular instruction. They frequently traveled the long journey to the mission chapel to make their confessions and receive Holy Communion.

The growing number of catechumens and baptized Catholics brought joy to the hearts of the missionaries, who had come such a great distance to bring the message of Christ to the Bantus* of central Africa. Not only were they pleased with the steady growth in numbers, but even more so with the sincerity and devotion with which these unusually intelligent men and women embraced the faith.

But a dark cloud soon filled the horizon and brought a temporary end to their labors. At the royal court, the French priests became the object of a secret conspiracy fomented by the Arabs. They were informed by some of their converts that they could be massacred at any moment, and that their assassins had already been selected.

The English missionaries stayed on in Uganda as they had not aroused the Arabs' enmity. However, Muhammed Ahmed's conquest of the Sudan cut off the Anglicans from the closest British military post, so they were completely removed from any intervention on the part of their countrymen. But an Arab *mullah* had come to the court and he and Mackay became good friends.

Nevertheless, the situation grew tense when the king decided to put his Christian subjects to a test; to prove whether they put their ruler or their new religion first.

* A broad term for a large number of linguistically interrelated peoples in central and Southern Africa.

Mutesa, at a gathering in the great audience hall, proclaimed, "As you know, my people have been terribly afflicted with the plague. I have been assured that this epidemic will come to a speedy end if we will all pray with the Arabs. Those present will leave the court at once and proceed to the mosque."

Father Lourdel was dumbfounded at this request, which could mean death to his Christian neophytes. He fell on his knees before the black ruler and cried, "I beg of you not to force your subjects to adopt any religion. God wants free service."

At this point the Arabs began to roar their disapproval, shouting, "Do not let this priest tell you what to do! The white men want to seize your country! They only want your subjects to follow their religion so as to get their support for France. Their religion is a religion of lies. There is no God but Allah, and Mohammed is his prophet!"

Father Lourdel realized the gravity of the situation and that what he did at this moment would determine the rise or fall of the Catholic faith in Uganda. He took the Gospels in his hand and proclaimed, "Let us ask God to judge between my religion and that of the Arabs. Have wood heaped up at the entrance to the audience hall. I will pass through as big a fire as you can burn, and I will walk through it with the Gospels in my hand. Let them do the same with the Koran. He whom the fire spares will certainly be the true messenger of God."

The Arabs were dumbfounded by this proposal and refused to accept the challenge. Father Lourdel had won the day. Seeing the Arabs back down, Mutesa declared that all at his court were free to choose their own religion.

The two English missionaries, Mackay and the Reverend Mr. O'Flaherty, hastened to congratulate

Father Lourdel and to thank him for what he had done for the Christian cause.

But in spite of his winning out in this particular predicament, Father Livinhac, the group's superior, could sense the temper of the times. It was not healthy for the Catholic priests to remain, nor for their followers who were in even greater danger. On November 8th, 1882, they and the children they had bought out of slavery departed for a new station on the south short of Lake Victoria in Tanganyika.

Father Lourdel had explained their departure to the *Kabaka* by saying that most of the priests were in ill health and needed a change of climate. Mutesa, rather than being angry, supplied the priests with canoes and men and even gave them a great ivory tusk weighing 140 pounds. Seeing them off was the sixteen-year-old Mwanga destined to be the next monarch. Standing on the shore with tears in his eyes as they pushed off in their canoes, Mwanga called to them, "Please come back."

The departure of the kindly White Fathers was viewed with great sorrow by the recently baptized Baganda, but it did not mean the end of Catholicism in Uganda. Bishop Lavigerie's program for training of catechumens had been long, thorough and hard, and now paid off. For, rather than dropping away from the faith when they were left without shepherds, these new Christians took over the work of catechizing and instructing the many young men at court who had shown a desire to embrace Catholicism.

In the royal enclosure itself, there were about one hundred and fifty adherents to the Catholic faith. And now in Buganda, there were four main areas of Catholic teaching. The royal palace itself where Joseph Mukasa became the chief shepherd and teacher also had as instructors Jean-Marie Muzeyi and, later,

Charles Lwanga. The outer courts and the area of the capital city were cared for by Andrew Kaggwa and the catechumen Mathew Kisule. Further away from the capital at the county seat of Ssingo, Mathias Kalemba and Luke Banabakintu taught the neophytes. In far off Bulemezi County the Christian postulants were instructed and led by Charles Lwanga. All of these leaders had been prepared by the fathers over a period of two years, and had expressed their faith by accepting baptism.

As the year 1883 wore on, King Mutesa became increasingly ill and tried various remedies, first of the Arabs, then the witch doctors. But nothing helped. On October 19th, realizing he was about to die, the *Kabaka* ordered everyone from the room except his two Christian attendants, Joseph Mukasa in whose arms he died, Jean-Marie Muzeyi and the princess royal. His last request showed that the influence of Christianity had not been lost upon the absolute monarch. It was that the mass slaughter that would usually accompany his passing should not be carried out. And so, with the close of 1884, came an end to the reign of Mutesa, the first king of Uganda to know and befriend the white man in this kingdom in the heart of Africa.

CHAPTER THREE

THE STORY
OF LITTLE KIZITO

The death of the king plunged the whole country into mourning. Meanwhile, a successor had to be chosen. By tradition the eldest son was not eligible. The second son had proven himself irresponsible by murdering his brother, so by process of elimination Prince Mwanga, then only eighteen, was chosen the new king.

The selection was not a good one, for Mwanga was young, restless, self-indulgent, addicted to smoking hemp and, worst of all, to the Arab-imported sodomy. Both Catholics and Anglicans wrote in letters to their superiors that the young monarch was highly unpredictable and capable of fearful revenge and rages.

Mutesa's body lay in state for five days, then amid pagan rites was buried in a coffin built by Mackay. It was committed to the ground in one of the largest houses of the royal enclosure at Nabulagala. Custom required that the next king commence his reign in a thoroughly new environment, with different supporters and pages, so the court was moved to temporary quarters at Budo.

There the new king was enthroned with extravagant ceremonies, the new sacred fuse was lit from which all sacred fires and ritual burnings proceeded. New appointments then had to be made at the conclusion of the protracted funeral rites.

Among these new appointments was Nyika, as guardian of the king's umbilical cord, one of the very highest ranks at court. Also, many more new pages were needed at this time. Nyika suggested the king allow him to send for his own adopted son, Kizito, a short, chubby lad of thirteen.

Also receiving one of the major new posts was a leading Catholic convert, Charles Lwanga of Bulemezi, who was made master in charge of the pages of the inner court. Naturally, little Kizito came under his direction and tutelage.

Kizito, destined to be the youngest of the martyrs, was born at Waluleta in the county of Bulemezi. His real father was Lukomera of the Lungfish clan; his mother, who bore nine children, was Wangabira of the Civet-cat clan. A blood pact had been made between the father of Lukomera and the father of Nyika, so when Nyika's father fell from favor and was exiled, the family of Lukomera supported and helped Nyika.

Later when Nyika's family was restored to favor, his father became county chief. He then showed his gratitude to the Lungfish clan by appointing Kizito's father to a chieftainship in his country.

At about this time Nyika decided to adopt Kizito, a son of Lukomera. Kizito's future suddenly looked very rosy when his adopted father was given the post next in

30

importance after that of chancellor. The young boy could expect rapid advancement, and soon he was appointed a royal page serving in the private quarters of the king.

He had already been exposed to the Catholic religion, as Nyika's natural son had been one of the first four men to be baptized at the Catholic mission in 1880. This young convert, Nalubwanda, led a group of neophytes and catechumens over the long dangerous route to the White Fathers' mission-in-exile in Tanganyika.

The day after his appointment as page, Kizito awoke and gazed sleepily at the grass roof overhead. Was not today something special, he wondered? Then, jumping up from his rough pallet, he remembered that this morning he was to depart for the new capital being constructed at Mengo. Only last evening, with the setting of the sun, the runner from court had arrived to announce that little Kizito had been greatly honored by an appointment to the palace as a royal page.

Kizito threw on his bark cloth toga and rushed along the path engulfed in thick green jungle foliage until he came to the river. Here he knelt down, splashed water on his face and rubbed his hands together with sand to thoroughly clean them. In an hour he was to leave! Nostalgia for his home and his foster mother stole over the boy, as he thought of the security of his life here in Bulemezi which he would now be leaving for the completely unknown world of the court. Oh well, he thought, most of the other pages will be new there, too, and we can become friends.

With this happy thought he returned to the larger hut of his foster mother, who had breakfast prepared and handed him the gourd bowl of *matoke*. She threw her arms about the small, excited boy and hugging him warned, "Remember, Kizito, my beloved, the king holds power of life and death over his subjects. You must always be loyal to your ruler and obey his every command. The new king has not had time yet to show us his nature, but whatever it is, you must be faithful and serve him to the best of your ability."

The young boy knelt down at her feet and kissed her hands warmly, for she had been very kind to him. "I promise that I will do my very best, so as to bring honor on my dear parents, and never shame them."

With this the youngster gathered up his few possessions, and trotted obediently behind the king's messenger as they set off along the jungle path to the new capital forty miles away.

The pair arrived at Dengo a day later, and Kizito was overwhelmed by what he saw. The vast enclosure built of elephant grass stalks seemed to stretch on endlessly. All around it, at intervals, burned fires carefully tended by palace guards.

The royal messenger led Kizito right through the main gate, past many huge thatched roof buildings, until they came to the very largest, the audience hall. Here the king was waiting to greet his new pages and assign them their duties.

Before entering, Kizito was met at the door by Joseph Mukasa, the majordomo of the pages, who put about Kizito's neck the cane necklace symbolic of his court position. Next he dressed him in the long, white cotton toga which hung from his right shoulder. The garment engulfed him and obviously was much too big. Kizito was younger and smaller than any of the more recent pages. Some laughed at him as he entered the great sixty-foot building tripping over his robe. "I will see that you have another one which fits," promised Joseph to the embarrassed youngster.

Quickly the new pages were assembled in a group and brought closer to the ivory throne on which was seated the new king of Uganda. All dropped to their knees and lay prostrate, their heads pressed tightly to the ground in the presence of their sovereign.

But curiosity got the better of Kizito, who raised his eyes just enough to glance at Mwanga for a second. What he saw was a short dark man, clad in a white tunic, with a circlet of lion's teeth about his neck and a red wool fez-like cap on his head. He had round, protruding eyes, high arched eyebrows, and a weak mouth which twitched in nervousness. Kizito ducked his head, when he saw the master of pages glancing at him.

The king waved his horsetail fly switch at the boys and cried, "Have them stand up. I wish to look over my new courtiers."

Joseph Mukasa gestured to his boys and they jumped to attention. "See, your majesty, what fine, young fellows we have brought together to attend to your every need." Then he introduced them to the monarch one by one.

Mwanga's eyes rested upon the angelic brown countenance of Kizito, and pointing his switch at him, asked, "Which one is he? That is the boy I desire for my personal page. See that he is sent to my private quarters at once."

Joseph knew instinctively that the beauty and youth of Kizito was what attracted him, and rushed off with the new page to warn him of the king's reason for his selection.

Taking him past the huge fence which enclosed the king's many wives, he led the youngster along a quiet, unused path to the anteroom. "Kizito, I must warn you

33

of the king. He desires young boys, as well as women, for the satisfaction of his lust. This is a terrible life for anyone to lead. I would hate to see a fine boy like you grow up in such an unnatural way. Also, I must tell you that I am a follower of Jesus. He does not approve such ways. So I will do all that I can to see that the king is satisfied elsewhere.

"Good master, I thank you," said the trembling boy. And Sir, "I have heard already from my uncle about the Lord Jesus Christ. Could you be so kind as to tell me more about Him."

"I would consider it a great joy and privilege," replied the tall master of pages. With that he led the beaming lad to the royal chambers to instruct him in his duties.

"First of all you are to run errands for your master, the king. Sometimes carry messages from one part of the palace grounds to another. Also, his majesty is very particular about the quality of meat used at his table. It will be your duty to collect and drive to the royal palace the cattle selected to be slaughtered for his use."

"I understand my duties, sir. Now will you tell me about Jesus?"

"This is rather a busy day for me with all the new pages," answered Joseph, "but if you desire to learn, you may come to the classes which I am giving every night. We meet in a special hut that King Mwanga built for our instruction classes. Ask one of the older boys to show you where it is."

"Do you mean that the new king is a Christian, too?" asked the amazed boy.

"No, he is not. But he is very interested in the religion of the French fathers, and has permitted me to instruct at court while they are away. When I am occupied with his majesty, you will find my assistant, Charles Lwanga, a very fine Christian and teacher. He will take care of you as he is in charge of the ten pages who wait upon the king."

In this way it came about that the young page began his instructions in the Catholic faith. Not under the care of the White Fathers, but rather with two of their most dedicated disciples.

Kizito was an apt pupil, and learned his lessons rapidly, but the greatest yearning of his heart was to see the holy men in white habits who had brought this beautiful faith to his country. On July 13th, 1885, his wish was fulfilled.

There had been a plot against the king, led by his pagan chancellor, Mukasa, who resented the fact that the Christian missionaries had been allowed in his country. Particularly that the young monarch joined them in the "Our Father" and assisted them in building their prayer houses. The old chiefs resented this threat to the ancient faith of their ancestors and decided to murder Mwanga and enthrone his brother in his place.

Word of the plot leaked out to Joseph Mukasa, the king's trusted friend and majordomo, who told him of the plot and thus saved his life. The king rewarded him by promising to make him the next chancellor. He likewise promoted many of the Catholics and Anglicans at the court, just to get even with the old pagan chieftains. The Catholics took advantage of Mwanga's new friendliness toward them by asking the return of the White Fathers to Uganda. They had been gone almost three years.

To demonstrate his good will, Mwanga sent a fleet of three hundred canoers to bring back Father Lourdel, Father Giraud and Brother Aman. Father Livinhac had traveled to Europe to be consecrated a bishop and would return immediately prior to the massacre, to be the first Catholic bishop of Uganda.

The French priests returned to a magnificent reception with rifle salutes, fireworks and crowds of enthusiastic new catechumens.

It was the custom when dignitaries arrived at Mengo, for the king to send groups of pages at intervals to greet them. And of course, one of the first to arrive, breathless and calling greetings, was Kizito. Bowing low before the white-clad fathers, Kizito shouted, "The *Kabaka* sends me to greet you. Welcome, welcome." No one could have meant it more from his heart than the little page, who knew that now at last he could see the wonder of wonders which Joseph and Charles had told him about, the Holy Mass.

Arriving at Mengo Hill, the French priests, surrounded by smiling throngs amid laughter and joyful greetings, went at once to the great audience hall where the *Kabaka* awaited them.

The moody monarch seemed almost glad to see the priests and greeted them graciously, making them promise never again to leave his country. The priests, as was the custom, gave the king a gift while he, in turn, granted them a plot of land at Rubaga only twenty minutes from the royal enclosure. The visit ended on a joyful note when the young monarch ordered three chiefs and their men to start work there on a mission building the very next day.

Standing by the priests at this moment was little Kizito. His bright eyes shone with excitement and anticipation as he thought of the happiness he would have in that new building, going there for instruction with the wonderful priests.

Mwanga then granted them complete freedom to teach the Catholic religion. Quickly the number of catechumens exploded to over eight hundred. Not all of these were at the court, but the message had been carried already by catechists to outlying villages, each of which already contained as many as fifty professing Christians.

However, not everyone was glad to see the priests return. The old chiefs resented the intrusion of the new religion and made no bones about it. The Frenchmen, in turn, could not feel entirely at ease in their pagan surroundings.

Yet the work of converting Ugandans must go on. When the French fathers announced the resumption of catechism classes, even more than before signed up.

The new mission building, built of reeds and roofed with traditional straw, was ready in a month. The small chapel was fitted out with many beautiful treasures that the White Fathers had brought with them by canoe, including a small statue of the Virgin Mary, their patron.

At court, Father Lourdel issued an invitation to any who wished to attend Solemn Mass the following Sunday for the dedication of the new chapel.

Kizito had been going regularly to the French mission for catechism classes and was overjoyed at the invitation. No one could imagine how much he wanted to go! But would he be allowed off from his duties?

The zealous youngster ran to his master, Joseph Mukasa, and pleaded for permission.

"Can I go? Can I go? Please let me off. I've never been to Mass, and now I can go!"

"Well, let me see," teased the tall chief of pages, towering over his smallest charge. "Won't you have to sweep the king's chamber that morning? And it seems to me that the butcher will want the cattle in the north field, and . . . ." But Joseph could no longer keep up the pretense to the earnest boy, whose mouth was trembling with disappointment.

"Yes, of course you can go! I will see that Mwuafu does your tasks for you. He is a Moslem, and will already have attended his services at the mosque on Friday.

"Thank you, thank you, kind master," cried Kizito, bowing his way out of the majordomo's presence.

On the following Sunday, Kizito did the most thorough job of bathing since he had left his stepmother's care. Wearing a shiny white toga, freshly washed in soap made of banana oil, he departed for the Catholic mission compound.

On the way he saw two other young pages ahead of him. Who might they be? Hurrying along he called in his high treble voice, "Wait up for me!"

The two lads, both about sixteen, came to a stop until Kizito caught up. "Mgaba! Denis! I did not know you, too, were Christians!"

"Oh, yes, young one. We have been studying with our master, Charles Lwanga, ever since he arrived at the court. He is the catechist for the pages of the inner chambers."

The three boys continued their walk to the compound chattering gaily until they arrived at the chapel, at the north end of the mission house. There they suddenly became very quiet and solemn.

Kizito had never been to Mass before so he watched the older boys enter and make the sign of the cross with the holy water at the door. Was it allowed for him to follow suit? Unsure, he abstained. He followed Denis into a bench at the back and knelt down to join him in a silent prayer.

When Kizito finally raised his head to look around, he thought he was in heaven. Everything was so beautiful! On the altar was a white and gold cloth hanging to the ground. At each end of the table were many brightly twinkling candles. In the center stood an ornate cross on which the tortured body of Jesus hung. Kizito could hardly bear to gaze upon the suffering of his beloved Lord. He looked to the side. The priests had brought a small carved statue of the Virgin Mary with them, and she stood smiling at Kizito from her pedestal.

Then a small bell tinkled in the distance and the three French Catholic priests of the mission entered through a side door to begin the service. Kizito was enthralled. Could these be the same men he had seen in their simple white habits at the court? Now they were arrayed in heavily embroidered vestments of gold and white in honor of the consecration of the new chapel. They looked grander than any kings the boys had ever seen at court.

Then the Mass began. Denis handed Kizito a book in which to follow the service. But it was too difficult. He could not read well as yet, and there was so much to watch. But, as it turned out, Father Lourdel read the text aloud in Luganda while the celebrant, Father Girault, recited the Latin in undertones. Kizito just reflected on the majesty and goodness of God in sending His beloved Son to redeem him.

A little bell rang again. Kizito had heard in catechism classes what this awesome moment was about. All bowed low in their places as the sacred moment of consecration took place. Then Father Lourdel held up the golden chalice containing the consecrated element, whereupon several men went forward to the altar rail to receive the blessed sacrament. Kizito's heart was filled with longing to be one with Jesus, like these baptized Christians. As they returned to their places, Kizito could see that they had experienced some great emotion. Their faces were aglow, almost transfigured.

Later, at the conclusion of Mass, when the priests stood outside the mission door to greet the catechumens, Kizito approached Pere Lourdel and asked, "Father, when may I be baptized, so that I can come to communion and receive God?"

Father Lourdel tried to be compassionate, but he alone knew how truly serious was the situation which existed for his Catholics at the court.

"Dear Kizito, I understand your yearning for baptism. It is a very healthy sign. However, you are so young, and also have had only a very short period of instruction. Our superior has given orders that none may be baptized until completing fours years of intensive training in our program.

"Four years! Why, father, I will be an old man by then! I may even be dead."

"Come now, Kizito, you are just a child still. The years will pass quickly."

Kizito turned away so the priest would not see him crying. He managed to whisper, "Goodbye, father. And thank you."

On his way back to the palace, while walking through the outer courts, Kizito passed right by another page just his size, who asked, "Friend, what is troubling you? You look so sad."

Kizito dried his eyes as surreptitiously as possible and stopped to see who had spoken. "My heart is so very heavy, I cannot even speak of it."

"Well, all right," countered the new boy, "but at least let me get you a drink of plantain juice. Perhaps then you will feel better. By the way, what is your name? I am Mubi."

"My name is Kizito, of the Lungfish clan. I am the king's personal page."

"Really! Well, then, that would explain why we have

not met before. I am assigned to the outer audience chambers. Besides, there are almost one hundred new pages. Come now, drink the juice."

Kizito held the clay vessel to his lips and said, "Mubi, you are a good friend—so kind."

"That is because I am a Christian. Would you not like to be a Christian, too?"

"Why, Mubi, I have never seen you at a catechism class, and I go regularly. When do you go?"

"That's funny, I have not seen you either! Many of us from the outer chambers go twice a week to the English mission for instruction."

"No wonder!" laughed Kizito, "I go to the French mission!"

The two boys hugged each other and laughed and laughed. "Then we are both Christians," said Kizito.

"Yes," replied Mubi. "See, here is my catechism book. I study it when I am off duty."

"And here is mine!" exclaimed Kizito, pulling out a small worn pamphlet from under his toga.

"Here, let us compare and see if they are the same." The boys exchanged instruction books, their curly black heads nodding up and down with the strain of deciphering the difficult Arabic characters.

"I cannot see that they are very different," shouted Mubi. "Let us be friends and Christians together!" And they left arm in arm.

CHAPTER FOUR

THE STORY OF MUBI

Mubi Nzalambi was a member of the Dogfish clan and, other than that, nothing is known about his parents, place of birth or childhood. When he arrived at the court of Mwanga as one of the newly appointed pages, he and his bosom companion, Wasswa, were assigned to the care of the prayer house which, at that time, was used as a mosque in the royal enclosure.

As this was situated in the outer courts, they came under the influence of Moses Mukasa. Moses, then about twenty-five years old and guardian of the prayer house, had been one of the first converts of the Anglican missionaries. Due to the tremendous size of the royal palace, which encompassed at least a square mile, it is easy to understand how the different areas might be divided into religious camps where the young pages would naturally fall under the influence of their supervisors, who were variously pagan, Moslem,

Roman Catholic or Anglican.

Most of the page boys assigned to work in the outer courts attended classes in reading and catechism at the English mission which at this point in the story had been established for six years with many converts and baptized members. It consisted of a sizeable chapel, a two-story mud-brick mission house built by Mackay, and the mission staff. There were thirty-five communicants.

Mubi soon could read the Luganda translation of Saint Matthew printed on the press Mackay had brought from England, and he knew much of the Swahili catechism by heart. He was nearly ready to be baptized when trouble suddenly descended upon the only two white men then present in Uganda, the Reverend Mr. Ashe and Alexander Mackay.

There had been a group baptism of a large number of Ugandans at the Anglican mission on Christmas Day, 1884. This was celebrated at a great feast that night with dancing and beating of drums and much hilarity. Mr. Ashe passed out candy to the young pages who were studying at the mission, and Mackay issued small paper prayer books to the older ones.

Such gaiety and merriment of large crowds of people could not pass unnoticed that close to the palace walls. The irate Moslems hurried to King Mwanga to tell him that many of his subjects would soon no longer be loyal to him, but turn their allegiance to the English. They prophesied that the British Empire would encompass his domain, as it had many others in Africa, and he would be deposed and worst of all a woman would succeed him, Queen Victoria.

Mwanga was furious, even a little frightened. He now sent spies to watch every movement of the English missionaries. In January, Mackay asked for permission to take the mission boat and sail down to the south shore of Lake Victoria in order to bring back supplies. There was another Anglican mission at Usambiro.

Mwanga suggested that Mackay take a legate from the court. Tired of being spied on, the missionary refused the offer, and made off with five of his mission boys to where he docked his boat on the lake.

The refusal to take the legate infuriated the king. Still worse, his Moslem chancellor quickly convinced the angry Mwanga to issue an edict forbidding any Baganda to work for the foreigners. Any found in their employ were to be arrested.

Ashe, Mackay and the five boys were intercepted on their way to the lake and ordered back to the capital. The wicked chancellor, Mukasa, informed the missionaries that they and their servants were under arrest for treason. He further accused the boys of trying to escape the country and emigrate to Tanganyika where it would be easier to practice their new Christian faith.

Ashe and Mackay argued fruitlessly through the night that they had no such plans. They had every intention of returning to Mengo. Mukasa ranted and raved that the Englishmen were liars and spies trying to infiltrate and take over Uganda for the British Empire.

Mr. Ashe replied, "We have no political ambitions here whatsoever. We wish only to take over the country for God. Is this a crime?"

The infuriated chancellor replied, "It is a crime to come here and try to convert the followers of Mohammed to your British religion. Africa should be under the cloak of Mohammed and I shall try my utmost to see that Mwanga and his court read the Koran, and not your Bible."

"Let me remind you," returned Ashe, "that we have never tried to convert any of the Arabs at court. Rather I have been a friend of your *mullah* since my arrival. Also, let me remind you that we are subjects of her majesty, Queen Victoria. She will avenge any injury to her countrymen where ever they may be stationed throughout the world. You had better release us at once."

Chancellor Mukasa, realizing the truth of this statement, allowed the missionaries to return to their houses, but stationed soldiers outside the compound walls preventing the entry of any native Christians.

As for the boys, they were detained on charges of trying to leave the country and were kept in the stocks until the following morning. Then the evil chancellor, desiring to put an end to the spread of Christianity at the court, prevailed upon the king to order them put to death as an example and warning to others.

Mr. Ashe, knowing the childishness of the African king, sent over a beautiful gift of silken cloth as a peace offering, asking the remittance of the sentence and release of the boys who were merely children.

Mwanga reprieved the two youngest, but turned the three others, Joseph Lugalama, eleven, Mark Kakumba, fifteen, and Noah Seruwanga, twenty, over to the executioner. All three of these boys had finished their catechism instruction and been baptized, which accounts for their biblical names. They were to become the first of many Baganda martyrs to die for their Christian faith.

The cruel chancellor, always thinking of ways to forward his own religion and deter Christians, next ordered all the young Anglican pages to watch the horrible death of their fellow Christians. Mubi was called to come to the execution site near the river

Mayamja, along with several other court pages, among them Freddy Kidza and Wasswa.

They watched while a low scaffolding was prepared on which the three martyrs were to be bound and slowly burned to death. But first the hefty executioner, his face painted horribly and his eyes bloodied from ritual plantain wine, approached the three youths with his great ceremonial hatchet flashing in the torrid sun. He raised it high and struck off their arms at each shoulder.

Then he threw the young boys, and their bloody arms onto the platform. Other executioners gathered fagots and lighting them, threw them under the platform. They soon turned the piled branches into a holocaust. Fortunately the wood was dry from a drought and the tortured writhings of the mutilated boys soon came to an end. Yet they could be heard singing a hymn over the crackling of the flames.

Chancellor Mukasa, standing by, made the most of the fearful situation. Turning to Mubi, who was crying into his white toga, already wet from the sweat of horror and fear, laughed at him, "Ah, so you are here, too. I will burn you and all the other page boys who go running to the mission. I know that you are a follower of Jesus."

Drying his face, young Mubi stood as tall as his fifteen years would permit and stated boldly, "Yes, I am. And I am not ashamed to admit it."

As Mubi returned slowly and sadly to the royal enclosure, the smoke could still be seen rising from the pyre where his former companions had become just a pile of ashes. Pondering in his heart the words of Mukasa, he wondered if, when his time came, he could be as brave. He now proposed to prepare himself by prayer and Bible reading for whatever might befall

47

him as a follower of Christ. He vowed never to renounce his faith.

Meanwhile back at the court, Joseph Mukasa, the devout Roman Catholic majordomo, tried to reason with the king and quiet him down enough, so that he would not injure the English missionaries. Joseph also petitioned the king to forgive Lady Sarah Kiyakule who had been imprisoned for teaching the women of the court the Anglican faith. Both she and her infant son had been condemned to be burnt alive with the three Protestant boys, but on learning that she was a relative of his, the monarch sentenced her to watch the execution so as to deter her from teaching the Christian religion to anyone else. Now he proposed to place her in his harem.

Although ill, she was being held in the stocks. Because the king loved Joseph and considered him his closest friend, he relented and ordered Lady Sarah released and turned her over to the English missionaries. Also, at the importuning of Joseph, he ordered the sentry guards away from the mission gate.

Once again the catechumens could come for instruction, although now it had to be stealthily, and only late at night. As soon as it seemed safe, Mubi and his friend, Wigram Kidza, both of whom had been witnesses to the martyrdom of their fellow churchmen, came by night to give a detailed report to their ministers.

The three missionaries were overjoyed to see them, and said they had been praying constantly for their safety, and that the anger of the king would be assuaged. They told the boys, "Our hearts have been nearly breaking at the thought of our dear, newly baptized boys dying such terrible deaths."

"Oh, no," exclaimed Mubi, "not horrible, but

glorious! You would have been so proud if you could have heard them. They were taunted by the chief executioner and his people on the way to the place of death. They shouted after them, 'You know Jesus Christ. You know how to read. You believe you shall rise from the dead? Well, we shall burn you, and see if it be so.'

"The three boys," continued Mubi, "answered not a word, but began to sing the hymn 'Daily, daily, sing the praises,' and, would you believe it, they continued singing even while the fire consumed them?"

Ashe could not contain his tears and commented on how proud and yet humble he felt to have baptized these martyrs. "At the same time," he remarked, "we must do everything in our power to avert any further such outbursts of insane anger on the part of the king. All of our lives are in his hands. Boys, you must stay away from the mission from now on, and continue your instruction as best you can under Moses Mukasa at the court."

"But Mr. Ashe" lamented Mubi, "how will I ever get baptized, and when can I make my first communion?"

"Although we have warned him not to come at this time, a bishop is on his way to Uganda. When he arrives and if the danger is past, we will baptize you. Later the bishop will confirm you, and then you will be able to make your communion."

"A bishop coming all the way from England! How good a man he must be to care for us so. I cannot wait to see him! When will he arrive?"

"We have no idea as yet, as it takes many months for mail to get here from England, and still many more for a bishop to travel to central Africa. But when he comes you shall be the first to know, and the first to be confirmed. Now run along my boys. It is very late, and no one is safe here, even at the mission."

The boys bade the missionaries goodnight, and walked by moonlight to the mud hut in the outer enclosure reserved for the pages.

That summer, the Roman Catholic priests returned from their three-year exile. The fickle Mwanga greeted them warmly, and said he was overjoyed that they had returned. As he was still angry with the English missionaries, he caused them even more unhappiness by pretending that he loved the French missionaries and would soon be baptized in the Catholic church. To the Frenchmen he granted complete freedom of movement and liberty to teach anytime, anywhere, even at court.

As the three Church of England missionaries and the four Catholic fathers were the only European Christians in the entire kingdom of Uganda, they felt they must present a united front, and help each other as much as possible through these difficult times. The chief enemy of both groups was the hate-filled chancellor, who still had hopes of making Uganda an Islamic nation.

It was shortly after the return of the French priests that Mubi and Kizito had met and begun their friendship. They would continue to be fast friends even to the end, when they died together in the fires of Namugongo the following year.

Both the Anglican and the Roman Catholic missionaries, realizing that they might have to flee the country at any moment, set up detailed plans for the spiritual care of their flocks. The leading baptized laymen of each denomination were chosen to continue teaching the many neophytes and catechumens and were authorized to administer baptism if there was immediate danger of death. A council of twelve lay leaders was chosen by the Anglicans including Moses, the chief of pages at the outer courts. Many Catholic laymen were authorized to continue the work of their denomination, among them Joseph Mukasa and Mathias Kalemba, both of whom had already done so during the three years when the priests had withdrawn from Uganda.

So both Kizito and Mubi were assured by their masters at court that no matter how bad the situation, they would be able to continue their instruction and eventually receive the sacrament of baptism.

Thus encouraged, the boys met soon afterward in the king's courtyard. "Say there, Mubi, have you heard about our new wrestling team?" Mubi fell into step beside Kizito and replied that he had not.

"Well, our chief page, Charles Lwanga, has started classes in wrestling, so we pages may have some form of recreation. They take place everyday after our catechism lessons. It is lots of fun, and many are enrolling."

"Kizito, do you think that Master Charles would let me attend?"

"I do not think so. Because you are not Catholic, and go to the Anglican mission."

"I do not mean the catechism classes! Just the wrestling."

The boys decided to walk down to the nearby lake together. They continued their chat as they padded along the fern carpeted path, shaded by the giant Muvule trees.

"Well, Mubi, I guess I could ask. Anyway, as I am the smallest page, there is never anyone my size with whom to practice. Since you are small like me, you would make a fine partner. Yes, I will ask."

On reaching the lake, glistening in the bright sunlight, they sat down on a dead log and tossed pebbles into the water.

"Mubi, do you remember the day we met, and I was so unhappy?"

"Why, of course I do," replied the handsome lad. "How could I forget!"

"Well, it seems that it may not be long before I am baptized, and then I will be able to make my communion. I am so happy these days."

"At our mission we also have good news. We have heard that a great bishop is coming all the way from England. Then I will be baptized and the bishop will confirm me, and then I, too, will be able to receive communion."

"We also are getting a bishop. Our Father Livinhac returned to France to be consecrated the first Catholic bishop of Uganda, and will be here soon again. I think I heard in January."

"Can you imagine! Two great bishops coming all this way to Africa for us. Is it not wonderful?" The two boys grabbed each other with delight and began wrestling on the soft lakeside beach, their black bodies turning grey as the sticky sand covered them from head to toe.

"Come, Kizito," warned the older boy, "we had better rinse off in the lake and return. It is an hour since we have attended to our duties and we will be scolded!" With that they dashed into the cool water, and then returned to the palace.

What Mubi had said about the Anglican bishop coming to Uganda was not only true, but happening at that very moment. James Hannington was born at Hurstpierpoint, Sussex, England in 1847, the son of a wealthy, titled landowner. His early years were spent in traveling and yachting aboard the family's several boats at the expense of his education, which was primarily by tutors—when they were available. Being of a high-strung and nervous disposition, he was generally in trouble with the masters at the Temple School which he attended during his teens in preparation for Oxford. Once he received twelve canings in a single day. But in spite of his run-ins with the faculty, he was very popular with his compatriots as he was quite athletic and utterly fearless.

His family had been nonconformist by tradition, but during his years at public school, his entire family took instruction and were confirmed in the Church of England. Following his graduation from St. Mary's College at Oxford, young James entered the family business, which he neglected for his very active social life among the elite of England, attending the horse races at Ascot, crewing for winning yachts, and climbing the Alps, each activity according to the proper social season.

But at the age of twenty-five, he suddenly had a change of heart and decided to study for the ministry, with the intention of carrying the message of Christianity to the poor and simple of England and, later, to the heathen, preferably in Africa.

At first no one took him very seriously, but he soon proved his true conversion to one and all. On his ordination, he went to a small country parish, where far from social pursuits of any kind, he devoted himself to the simple fishing folk, sitting all night in the cottages of the sick and dying to bring them what comfort he could, both spiritually and physically. Having a slight knowledge of medicine, he was a sort of free country doctor.

After this apprenticeship, he was called to the parish church in his hometown of Hurstpierpoint. Here the people received the son of their wealthy landlord with the greatest respect and love, hanging on every word he uttered from the pulpit as from the mouth of God. No minister anywhere could have received greater love and more faithful attendance.

In spite of the happy circumstances of his parochial duties, his thoughts turned continually to mission work in Africa to which he felt the strong call of God. When Hannington read of the murder of the two young missionaries, Smith and O'Neil, on the shores of Lake Victoria, he immediately felt compelled to go in their places.

On May 17th, he sailed as the head of a mission party of six for Zanzibar, and from there overland to Uganda. However, he was unable to complete the journey, being prostrated by fever and dysentery. He was carried to the coast by porters and made sport of his sufferings in gay little drawings of his jouncing ride in the litter from which he was several times tossed into rivers, once nearly into the gaping mouth of a hippo.

Requiring expert medical attention and a long recuperation, he was sent home to England, but only after the promise that he could return to his now beloved Africa as soon as he had fully recovered.

Because of his executive ability and knowledge of the area and and its languages, in June of 1884 he was consecrated bishop of Eastern Equatorial Africa in elaborate ceremonies at Lambeth Palace. But not until 1885 was he able to begin his return trip to Africa, leaving in England his dear wife and four little children. This time he planned to take a different route which had been used only once previously and was named after its originator, the explorer Joseph Thompson. This was reputed to be much shorter. Leaving from Mombasa and traveling northwest through Masai country directly to the northern part of Uganda, Hannington avoided the long journey around the lake, the route he had undertaken previously. Former missionaries had not used Thompson's route because of the aggressive nature of the fierce Masai.

Unknown to the bishop and his party of fifty-three bearers and one other white man, a Goan cook, there was a legend or superstition among the Baganda that strangers entering their country by the northern route through Busoga country would one day conquer Uganda. The bishop had unfortunately chosen the very route which the former King Mutesa had called "entering the country through the back door."

As soon as Mr. Mackay learned of the bishop's intended route, he hastened to warn him that he would offend the king by coming that way and would place himself and his entire party in danger of death. But the bishop had already left Mombasa. He never received the warning.

As mentioned previously, James Hannington was a man who was utterly fearless. The approaching journey through Masai country excited him rather than caused him any apprehension. As a young man he had been very fond of spelunking, and had several times been nearly drowned when the caves he was exploring were filled with water as the tide came in.

In addition, he had been a great lover of hunting. This favorite hobby had caused the loss of his left thumb. At the age of twelve he blew it off with explosives he was holding while hunting ducks. However, this maiming in no way hindered his activities, and was instrumental in helping to positively identify his remains following his martyrdom.

At the time of his last expedition, the Germans occupied the port of Bogamoyo and their forces were stationed all along the usual trail through Tanganyika.

The bishop, fearful the Germans would prevent his passing through there, chose the alternate northwestern route directly to the shores of Lake Victoria.

He sent a letter to the English missionaries in Uganda requesting them to meet him in early October on the north shore of the immense lake, then to take him via mission boat to the capital of Uganda which was then situated at Dengo.

On September 25th, Ashe and Mackay went to court with a gift of cloth for the king and requested permission to take the mission boat to meet the bishop who was on his way to the court from England.

The black monarch asked if the white man would be bringing him many presents.

Mr. Ashe replied, "He will not come empty-handed. But he is a great chief, not of this world's goods, but of religion. He is a great teacher."

"Perhaps he is a great warrior," countered the wily king. "How am I to know that he is not coming to take away my country?"

Mr. Mackay replied, "He is a minister like Mr. Ashe. He is not a man of war but of peace. He comes only to tell you about Jesus Christ and to confirm those who have been baptized.

At this point the king waved the Englishmen away, and when they had left, called together his chancellor and chiefs. Addressing them he said, "All white men are the same, taking away the African's nations one after the other. This is one of their chiefs and he comes to attack us. We must get him first."

But Kulugi, the court treasurer, was the only one who kept his head in this overwrought, emotional situation. He proposed that a legate be sent ahead to the bishop's party to tell them not to come by way of

Busoga. He recommended they proceed first to Musalala at the south of the lake, which was two hundred miles long, and wait there until the king gave them permission to come to the capital.

A young Protestant, by the name of Micah Sematimba, was chosen to go as legate and carry the message to Bishop Hannington. Meanwhile the mission boat set out October 1st to meet the prelate. Nothing further occurred, and things settled down into their usual routine until the morning of Sunday, October 25th. A Protestant page, Gideon Entanda, brought news to the court that two Englishmen and twenty porters had arrived at the headquarters of Luba, a great chief in Busoga.

King Mwanga immediately called together his councilors and chiefs to discuss the situation. The wicked chancellor began a tirade, shouting that the English intruders should be put to death and all their luggage seized, expecting that they would have much of value.

The king, after a long discussion, finally agreed and ordered a band of armed men to leave at once for Busoga. All the chiefs shook their spears in agreement and hastened to call their warriors together to depart.

One of the pages present during the discussion was Kasamitala, one of the chancellor's own sons. He ran at once to tell his companions that the king had ordered the death of the Anglican bishop. On hearing this dread news from one of his closest friends at court, Mubi felt it must be true, and left stealthily by night for the house of the English missionaries. Mr. Mackay was in bed with a fever, but came downstairs to hear the dread story from Mubi. The three Englishmen were shocked and horrified, but still had hopes that it might not be true.

Mr. Ashe, who was in good health, hurried over to the Catholic mission to tell the White Fathers, and ask their help. Father Lourdel suggested that they write another letter telling the bishop to come the southern route so as not to antagonize Mwanga. On Monday morning, the priest hurried off to the king to beg him to reconsider his decision to kill the bishop. After many entreaties, Lourdel finally got Mwanga to promise that he wouldn't hurt Hannington.

But, of course, the king could not keep such a promise. It was already too late to contact his forces and countermand his order. But he continued to maintain the pretense.

All the negotiations had, indeed, been in vain from the start. Bishop Hannington, his cook, and all of his bearers died at Busoga on Thursday, October 29th. Details of the hideous murder came back to the sorrowing missionaries in fragments. One of the Anglican pages, Musoke, had been an eyewitness to the massacre and provided them with most of the information.

The bishop's party had arrived at Busoga, on the northeast shore of Lake Victoria, on October 21st. Chancellor Mukasa and his men arrived and arrested them the evening of October 27th. The bishop was tied up and confined in a dirty hut filled with cobwebs and rats. When the prelate complained that he was ill, they built him a new hut. The local chief, Luba, brought his wives—they numbered in the hundreds—to stare at the captive white man. The next day, Wakoli, the king's gatekeeper, arrived with orders confirming the death sentence.

The entire party was taken to an open place outside the plantation, where fifty of the African porters were speared to death. Three escaped because they had been chosen for slaves by the local chief as payment for his part in the affair.

When the bishop realized that he was to be killed, he asked to be shot rather than speared. But his final request was ignored. Two hefty warriors ran their spears deep into his body. The bishop's last words were "Tell the *Kabaka* that I have purchased the road to Buganda with my death. I have died for your people."

The body was not yet cold when the warriors severed Hannington's head and feet, and left his bleeding corpse for the hyenas. They believed such mutilation would keep the Christian from arising from the dead and coming back to wreak vengeance on his murderers.

The chancellor and his warriors waited six days after the massacre before returning to the court. It was then that Mwanga's page, Kasamitala, who had accompanied his father, the callous chancellor, on the fatal journey, conveyed the tragic story to the heartbroken missionaries.

Their first thought was for the safety of their flock. With such a turn of events, the king would continue to be in a dangerous mood, and very likely would kill them, along with their catechumens and Christian pages.

Mr. Ashe sent away all their houseboys to hide among Christian friends. Mr. O'Flaherty carried out the plans set up earlier to initiate services in the homes of their ten native elders, rather than have converts come to the Anglican mission in great crowds and attract the anger of the king.

The king was angry! He was almost in a frenzy. The English missionaries had been advised by one of the princesses to bring him a gift, which was the customary way after the execution of a loved one to show no ill feelings were harbored against him.

King Mwanga was operating under the delusion that

no one knew of the murder of Bishop Hannington, that in fact it had never happened.

But, on receipt of the gift, he sensed immediately that the missionaries had been told of the terrible deed. Someone had leaked the information.

The *Kabaka* called for both the Catholic and Anglican missionaries to come to court on November 11th. He let loose with all sorts of vilifications and accusations, storming at them with his wildly protruding eyes.

Pointing at them, he shrieked, "What double-tongued boys here have been telling you my secrets? Who are your informants? Tell me or I shall put you in the stocks!"

The missionaries remained outwardly calm and declined to name any names.

The king kept up the tirade for two hours until Mackay, who was shaking with fever said, "You know that we came repeatedly to court to see you, and you refused to receive us. The gift was to soften your heart, so that we might speak to you. Are you angry with us? What have we done?"

"My boys go to your place, supposedly to learn to read, and what do you do? You turn them into spies against their own king! You have wrested even my darkest secrets from them with your sorcery. I will kill anyone found at your mission station! Do you understand? And when I find out who is your informant, I will have him put to death."

With that, the stormy audience at last came to an end. But in spite of all the king's threats, the Christian pages continued to come to the missionaries by night, including Mubi, who realized that now he could not be confirmed and that communion might be forever out of his reach.

CHAPTER FIVE

JOSEPH MUKASA BECOMES
THE FIRST CATHOLIC MARTYR

Back in London, the Church Missionary Society surveyed its work in central Africa to date and realized that most of the fine, highly educated and dedicated men whom they had sent out to the Lake Victoria region had died, four from fever, three speared to death, and two from accidents. The mortality rate was frightful. Yet Alexander Mackay had survived it all. Of the original eight sent on the Uganda mission, he alone remained alive. This dedicated engineer, still in his twenties, seemed to have a special protection from God. Also, his engineering talents helped to bring more Baganda to Christ than the teaching of the clergy.

Mr. Mackay could build houses and piece together a steam engine carried in small sections the eight hundred miles from Zanzibar to the lake. Because of Mackay, the missionaries had a steamer for transportation on the lake.

Also, Mr. Mackay could carve letters in Luganda from which he printed material so the courtiers and chiefs could learn to read. On his printing press, he made copies of the Gospels in their native language for Mwanga and his people. Mackay could do anything, but in particular among the Englishmen sent to Uganda, he seemed able to survive.

He himself had no illusions of immortality, however, for in a letter to his father soon after the murder of Bishop Hannnington, he wrote, "We ourselves are in a position of great danger. We are suspected of political aims, and are called spies and pioneers of invasion. Our pupils are believed to be won over to English rule, and to be false to their country. All are thus suddenly dispersed. We have written a letter to Sir John Kirk (the consul at Zanzibar) to request this king to let us leave in peace. But meanwhile it is dreadful suspense to have, as it were, a sword continually over one's head. The chancellor continues to be our worst enemy, and recently we discovered a plot on the part of the king and head chiefs to kill us all.

"The king's own favorite page, the head of the personal servants, ventured to say to him one day that it was wrong to kill the bishop, as white men came only as benefactors of the country."

This favorite page was none other than Joseph Mukasa, who had started out as a catechumen at the Anglican mission in the days of Mutesa. There he had learned to read and write and became an assistant catechist to the English missionaries.

But on the arrival of the French Catholics, like several others, he decided he liked the teaching of the White Fathers better, and began instruction at their chapel. Joseph had been one of the first among his people to be baptized by the Catholic missionaries on April 30th, 1882, and had been in complete charge of the instruction of all Catholic pages at court during the three year absence of the White Fathers from Uganda.

All during this period, he increased in holiness of life, meanwhile becoming the new king's closest confidant and friend. The *Kabaka* seemed ever more friendly toward the Catholics, while his anger mounted steadily against the English, who now despaired of their lives in the fierce air of animosity which surrounded them. It was Joseph who had advised the king to send for the White Fathers to return to Uganda and now he took it upon himself to reprimand Mwanga for killing Bishop Hannington, thereby endangering his position at court, and worse yet, his life. He also incurred the wrath of the many chiefs who still held to the old pagan ways of witchcraft and taboos. Hearing one of the mediums beating a drum and reciting incantations in the palace courtyard, Joseph sent some of his older pages to beat him up. They did so, and scattered his little bag of amulets and fetishes all over the ground.

But even more dangerous was his protection of the young Catholic pages from the king's practice of sodomy. This vice had been brought to court in the preceding century by the Arabs and had a great hold upon the ruling element. But it was strictly forbidden by both Catholic and Anglican missionaries.

Joseph did all in his power to guide and protect his young charges under these difficult circumstances. He instructed them that the ordinances of God must always comes first even before the wishes of their king. He urged them never, even if it cost them their lives, to give in to the evil demands of the *Kabaka* and his vicious companions. He advised and urged, "When the king solicits you for evil, refuse." To avoid these situations, Joseph would send off on an errand any page who had obviously been called to the king's chamber for these purposes.

He even had the courage to reprimand the king in public. "Do not act like that, my master," he would say. "I beg and implore you do not act like that, because God detests uncleanness. Leave my children alone, and rather leave to the Moslems the vileness with which Satan inspires them."

Naturally, the king's liking for Joseph grew cool, and now gave place to violent anger, as he once more publicly reprimanded his king on the subject of Bishop Hannington. "My king, you did wrong to put the English bishop to death. Your father, Mutesa, never harmed any white men, and would not have done such a terrible deed." This last was too much. The king exploded.

He called Joseph to come close, and then began to upbraid him. He threatened to exterminate all Christians, and especially to begin with him. Without stopping to eat or sleep he heaped abuse upon his old friend and majordomo throughout the long night, not letting him go until the dawn rose in a red haze over the bottle green hills of Kampala.

Joseph, sensing that his days were numbered, walked down in the eerie red glow, to the Catholic mission where he attended Mass and received his last communion from the hands of Father Lourdel. On leaving the church, he was stopped by little Kizito who came running up to him, crying and panting. "His majesty wishes to see you at once. Run away, dear master, for I fear for your life."

The handsome majordomo patted the young page's curly head and replied, "Come now, Kizito, the king and I are very good friends. Have no fear."

But Kizito had been at court attending the king while Joseph was at Mass. He had overheard the conversation between Mwanga and his pagan chiefs

64

who wished to do away with the Catholics' lay leader.

"No! No! dear teacher, you do not understand," continued the desperate boy, tugging at Joseph's hand to prevent him from going on to the palace. "I heard the king say he would do away with you because you are trying to destroy him. He called you a vicious snake and said it was you who arranged for the white bishop to come by way of Busoga."

"Kizito, that is foolishness! I have nothing to fear."

"Oh, yes you do! You do! The chancellor, who hates you because you have taught his own son the Christian religion said, 'Give him to me, I will get rid of him.' I know they plan together to kill you. Please run away."

The tall fellow just laughed, and gripping the boy's hand tightly in reassurance said, "What sort of a teacher and example would I be to run away from death. Rather would I seek it, if it is to be for Christ. I am not afraid and I don't want you to be either." Reaching the little hut where he slept, Joseph said, "Let us kneel here together and pray, my little one, for strength and courage for the ordeal which awaits us."

While Joseph and Kizito were praying, two men came to take Joseph as a prisoner before the *Kabaka*. They tied his hands behind his back and led him to the audience hall.

Jeeringly, the king turned to his Moslem chancellor and said, "You have saved me from this sorcerer. Now there will no longer be two *Kabakas* at this court!"

Facing the prisoner kneeling before him, the chancellor added, "So this is the fellow who always wanted to teach me and told me to put away my charms. Well, away with him. Burn him in the fire."

"So, I am to die for my religion," calmly stated the man who had been the court favorite of two kings.

"That is it exactly," replied Mwanga, and turning to the executioner commanded, "Take him to the courthouse at the entrance gate and fetch firewood to burn him."

The martyr was now led away while the chief executioner went off to arrange for the firewood. Mukajanga, wearing the grass wig symbolic of his awesome position returned with his assistants, all carrying bundles of firewood which were piled up near the gate for the sacred fire. Mukajanga, out of respect for their long standing friendship, ordered an assistant to untie Joseph's bonds.

Joseph thanked him, saying, "That's right to do. I am dying for my religion. You need not be afraid that I will escape. Tell Mwanga that he has killed me for no reason, but I forgive him. I will plead for him at the tribunal of God."

Kizito, Mark and Nikodemo had followed the martyr to the execution site, their faces drawn with sorrow, tears streaking their dusty faces. But Mukajanga drove them off shaking his amulets at them and, shouting, "Off with you! Do you want to make a king of him?" The three scampered off and returned to town where they went straight to the French mission to tell Father Lourdel the horrible news.

The priest was hurrying off to the palace to beg Mwanga for the life of his finest Christian assistant, when he saw rising from the hollow below Mengo Hill the smoke which could be nothing else but the funeral pyre of Joseph Mukasa. As his errand was now hopeless, the dejected party of priest and pages returned to the mission, where the kindly young priest did his best to comfort the forlorn trio.

"Father, what will we do now without our beloved Joseph?" asked Kizito.

"First we must pray for him, and for the king to embrace our faith, so this persecution can end. But at

66

court, not all has ended for you. Charles Lwanga, the head page of the inner court, will take over your direction and care for you just as Joseph did. Do not despair, my boys, all will be well."

Joseph died on November 15th, 1885, the first of the twenty-two Catholic martyrs of Uganda. The chief executioner, feeling pity for his old friend ordered his head chopped off just as the sacred flame was touched to the low wooden platform on which Joseph was tied. He at least was spared the long, slow death which his fellow Christians would later suffer at Namugongo.

Only a few minutes after his headless corpse was consumed by the roaring flames, the fickle king sent a little page running to the execution site shouting, "Reprieve! Reprieve! The king has forgiven him!"

But it was too late. Mwanga's favorite, who had died with words of forgiveness for the monarch on his lips, was past saving.

The following day, while the many frightened pages of the inner court pressed around him for advice and encouragement, Charles Lwanga, the head page now, and the finest wrestler at court, suggested to the boys that they have a match to take their minds off the horror of the past days.

The youngsters tried grappling each other, but their hearts were not in it. "Master, how can we play when our hearts are so heavy?" asked Kizito.

"A Christian is gay and happy no matter what the circumstances," answered Charles, who was now their instructor, although at twenty-five, not many years older than they.

Denis, who was only sixteen, said, "If we are to die, I could do so much more bravely and gladly if I were baptized." Turning to his fellow pages, the boy asked, "Wouldn't you, too? Let us go to the mission and ask Father Lourdel to baptize us."

With Charles Lwanga in the lead, the entire group of Catholic pages trooped off to the new mud-brick mission house of the White Fathers.

Here Charles presented their case and the great likelihood that they might all be called on to die for their faith. "Baptize us, father," he asked. And they all chorused, "Baptize us, father, before we die."

Under such circumstances, and knowing that some of them had been under instruction for many years, how could the good priest deny them? Immediately Father Lourdel went into the tiny sacristy, put on his surplice, and stole, and returned to stand before the tin basin which served as a font.

Before starting the service he asked Charles and Denis and several others who were to be baptized many questions to satisfy himself that they were adequately prepared. In each case he could tell from their answers that they knew the catechism by heart, understood the nature of the sacraments, and were fully aware of the seriousness of the step which they were about to take. Then he instructed each candidate to step forward, and pouring water over the bowed wooly head, intoned solemnly, "I baptize thee in the name of the Father, Son, and Holy Ghost."

Then, late that night, after all had made their first confession, Mass was said and the new Christians made their first communions.

All the following week, the catechumens at court, sensing their days were numbered, came stealthily by night, slipping through the priests' banana patch and sliding under a break in the reed fence to the mission. The king had already forbidden anyone to go there on pain of death. The fathers spent every minute instructing and then baptizing these brave young people, who were willing and prepared to die for their faith. By the end of the week, over one hundred and five had been made members of Christ through baptism, many of them soon to be added to the roster of saints through another baptism—of fire.

But poor little Kizito was still not numbered among those baptized at the mission. No matter how hard he importuned the priest, Father Lourdel repeated that he was too young, and not sufficiently prepared. "Please, father," he begged once more. "I will die without baptism, and not be allowed into heaven."

"Do not worry," countered the priest. "Things have quieted down at the court. You have nothing to fear now." And he ushered him out of the unglassed window of the mission.

Mubi had also been many times by night to the English missionaries and received the same story. The only clergyman there in November, 1885, was the Reverend Mr. Ashe. He and Mackay had selected a number of outstanding laymen to form a church council, and it was in the homes of these men that the Anglicans gathered for instruction and fellowship.

Not long after the king announced that no one might go near the Anglican mission on pain of death, Ashe and Mackay received a message that the young admiral of the canoe fleet, Gabunga Kijambu, wished to see them.

He had been reading the Scriptures with them and attending their services for some time, and now, in the note, he was asking to be baptized. The missionaries were delighted but also alarmed. It was a dangerous time. For that reason they conducted the meetings for instruction prior to baptism as well as baptisms themselves (five others had also asked to be baptized at this time) at the house of the local blacksmith.

That same week, Mr. Mackay completed printing of 350 copies of Saint Matthew's Gospel in Luganda. They would be distributed in exchange for food and other commodities.

Then the diary of Bishop Hannington came into their hands. Mwanga's agents had brought it back from the site of the massacre in Busoga. An Anglican convert had purchased it in turn and presented it to Mackay. They read the miniscule scratches with intense interest. It ended with a brief note on October 29th, the day of the bishop's murder, and showed that he had suffered terribly with the fever as well as imprisonment during his last days.

Mackay and Ashe forwarded the diary on to the bishop's widow who turned it over to his biographer, E.C. Dawson, who saw it into print the next year. His book, *James Hannington, A History of His Life and Work, 1847-1885,* went through at least six editions in Great Britain and was also heartily received by American readers after its publication in New York in 1887.

Shortly prior to all of this, Mr. O'Flaherty had finally received permission from the king to return to the coast. Glad to leave Mengo where their missionary endeavors were so much curtailed, he was at the same time sorry to leave the two men with whom he had shared so many months of hardship and anxiety. As it turned out they were never to see each other again, as O'Flaherty died of a fever while aboard ship on the Red Sea.

Next followed a period of relative peace and safety, during which the work of the Catholic and Anglican missionaries continued, though much restricted, by stealth and at night, each mission reporting that "many have been baptized."

CHAPTER SIX

THE COURT
MOVES TO MUNYONYO

Christmas of 1885 passed relatively quietly, with services at both missions well attended. The king's attention was temporarily turned toward Bunyoro, where his armies had gone to do battle with their neighbors to the north. These petty wars were the main occupation of the men of Uganda, who left farming duties to their many womenfolk. Also, the bounty brought back from these regular forages was easier to come by than earning it by the labor of their backs.

Victorious warriors customarily stole everything moveable, killed all the men, burned down what was left of the villages, and carried off the women and children as slaves.

However, Mwanga's troops returned with a sorry tale to tell their monarch. The commander-in-chief had been killed, many of his favorite warriors left behind dead, and even worse, there was no bounty! The new year of 1886 was off to a poor start.

Then in February, more ugly incidents occurred to increase the bad temper of the king. At eight o'clock on the evening of February 22nd, King Mwanga and his chiefs were drinking and singing in the beer house, when suddenly a great explosion shook them off their seats.

The sky was lit up with a great flash of light while orange flames filled the night air over the whole of the palace. The straw huts, fanned by the winter wind, caught fire in an instant, and spread rapidly from one palace building to the other with a great whoosh as each flimsy building of weeds and straw burst into a ball of fire. Chiefs and slaves ran screaming from the blazing buildings, their flaming cotton or bark cloth togas burning the skin from their bodies.

In the beer hall, the chiefs ran about wildly until they realized that they had not been hurt. The king was the first to exit the building screaming, "The English have come to avenge their bishop. We are surrounded." Then he ran to his private apartment, snatched up a sword and raced all the way to the Catholic mission where he asked for refuge.

Father Lourdel, who had been hurrying to the scene of the fire to try to give assistance to the injured, passed him on the way and tried to calm his fears. He reassured Mwanga that the English were not coming, and suggested to the chiefs that they take their king to the prime minister's house.

The next day, while Mwanga was still recuperating from his fright of the night before, an electrical storm came up. Great shafts of lightning struck haphazardly over what was left of the mile-wide enclosure. Suddenly a forked streak of the "fire from heaven" pointed straight at the house where the firearms and gunpowder were stored. This time there was an even worse explosion as 100 kegs of gunpowder blew up. The intense heat and fire spread to the few buildings which remained, and by morning the king's palace, which formerly had encompassed a square mile, was leveled to the ground.

The quaking monarch, product of a pagan culture, feared this was a warning from the gods of Uganda that he had done wrong in befriending and harboring the alien Christian religion at his court. Mengo, a smoldering ruin, existed no more. Also, all of his treasures, his arsenal, and many of his best chiefs had perished in the conflagration.

About eight miles away at Munyonyo was a small hunting lodge near Lake Victoria where the king and his favorite courtiers liked to go to hunt the mammoth hippos who wallowed on the shores. The *Katakiro* (chancellor) now suggested that the king and some of his favorite pages move there temporarily while the palace was being rebuilt.

This seemed an excellent plan, and after making up a few bundles of what was left of his former immense fortune, the king and his party departed. Hearing of the king's new state of penury, the Anglican missionaries went immediately to visit him and took a present to somewhat make up for his losses.

Mwanga accepted the gift, but refused to see the white men whom he declared had bewitched him and caused the fire from the sky. He announced that they would be the death of him. Each day after that, Mwanga became more and more disagreeable. One morning he ordered Mackay to bring his mission boat to a certain spot on the shore. Then he sent his executioner to capture him and cut off his head.

Mubi overheard the plot and, accompanied by Wasswa, scurried by night the eight miles back to the mission to warn Mr. Mackay of the king's plot.

Even more disasters were to occur before the situation came to its bloody conclusion. Another fire struck, burning the queen mother's palace to the ground. Shortly thereafter, one of the king's canoes overturned, sending crew and cargo to the bottom of the lake.

This succession of unhappy events was used as fuel by the Arabs and pagans at the new court to turn the king against the unfortunate Christians. Into the monarch's ear, the *Katakiro* now whispered, "The Christians are the cause. The gods are angry."

The Arab *mullah*, standing before the ivory throne and looking very pious with his hands folded in his sleeves, bowed low and said, "The Christians are obviously sorcerers using their God to destroy our country."

Mwanga wailed, "It is true! They make their God do whatever they want. When they took me for a friend, they prayed to Him for me and all went well. Now they ask Him to destroy me, and you see what is happening!"

The *mullah* hissed, "You must get rid of them at all costs." When the white men have taught all these children to despise and disobey you they will be the masters of this country not you. The king looked at all the small brown faces of his pages turned toward him in trust and affection. He wondered how he could destroy these young boys. Who would be the next chiefs if all these fine young pages were killed? No, he thought, there must be another way. Addressing them firmly, he commanded, "If you do not stop praying and running to the white missionaries, I will kill you all."

The youngsters looked toward their leader, Charles Lwanga, who was the embodiment of prudence, kindness and courage. He would tell them what to do. They had complete faith and trust that all would be well.

Now unable to go to either mission house, the young pages turned to their leaders for prayer services and instruction. The Catholics, having lost their blessed Joseph Mukasa through martyrdom, went to his successor, Charles Lwanga, while the Anglican boys turned to Moses Mukasa, a council member authorized to teach them.

Naturally they had to pray in secret, and usually met late at night. As a consequence, the little fellows went about their court duties practically dragging their feet from lack of sleep.

Mwanga suspected that something of the sort was going on behind his back, but being moody, he changed his likes and dislikes from day to day, and shortly his temper cooled off somewhat.

But the following week a letter arrived from the coast written by the British consul of Zanzibar protesting the murder of Bishop Hannington. Feeling guilty again, and furious that news of his bloody crime had come to light and was common news all over Africa, Mwanga flew into a rage. He imprisoned three Catholic guards at the palace, fearing that they would allow any British who came to capture him to enter the court.

On the Saturday before Easter, he again proclaimed from his throne that Christianity was forbidden in his nation, and all practicing Christians were to be seized.

In spite of this dire warning, a dozen catechumens were baptized that night at the Catholic mission, while the Anglican, Mackay, reported in his diary on Easter Sunday, April 25th, 1886, that twenty-five people altogether partook of the Lord's Supper, "some of them for the last time."

But the Catholic baptism only served to anger the king still further, for among the candidates was his older sister, the Princess Nalumansi.

She had for several years attended classes at the Anglican mission where she was eventually baptized. Princesses in Uganda were forbidden to marry, but she defied this ancient tradition by falling in love with Joseph Kaddu, a Catholic baptized in 1880. Both of these Christians now asked to be joined in holy matrimony. They were married in the Catholic chapel with a special dispensation for a mixed marriage. Then, a few days later, on Easter Saturday, she was received into the Roman Catholic church, taking the name of Clara.

All might have gone well if the king had not appointed her guardian of the tomb of the late King Jinja, Mwanga's grandfather.

That May, Princess Clara and her new husband left to take up residence in Luwunga at the house attached to the nearby royal tomb. Finding her predecessor's grass hut filled with amulets, fetishes and charms, the princess threw all these satanic implements into a pile and made a bonfire of the lot. Then she drove away the witch doctor in attendance at the shrine.

As if this were not enough to anger the pagan gods, and bring grief upon the entire nation, she next took her umbilical cord, an object of veneration for all members of royalty, cut it up in little pieces, and buried them in the ground.

In the eyes of her peers and countrymen these actions were shocking beyond belief, and bound to bring upon all of Uganda the wrath of the outraged pagan gods. The news of this frightful sacrilege sped fast throughout the country causing consternation and fear that some terrible calamity would befall all Ugandans at any moment.

The king went into a rage, but did not dare to harm a member of the royal family. Instead he vented his fear and wrath on those closest to him, the fifty or so pages who had accompanied him from Mengo to the temporary residence at Munyonyo. Ordinarily, there were as many as five hundred young sons of chiefs and other leading personages serving their royal master's needs. But the small court at Munyonyo had limited sleeping quarters making this large number unfeasible.

Charles Lwanga had been very successful in protecting his young Christians from the unnatural advances of the venal king. But he did not take it upon himself to protect any others. As a result, Mwanga had been indulging his homosexual practices with Mwafu, the pretty young son of his own *Katakiro*, Mukasa, a follower of Mohammed.

Mwafu was a member of the Bahima race who may have immigrated centuries before from Abyssinia. He was handsome, lighter skinned, with a fine straight nose and thin curved lips. He could not fail to attract the licentious monarch with his frail beauty, and had given him many nights of pleasure, resulting in even more power to the boy's father.

But on May 25th, the beginning of the great persecution, Mwanga had gone to the huge inland sea to hunt. When he returned to shore wishing for immediate care of his wants and comforts, not one of his large retinue of pages was in sight. "Where are my boys?" shouted the angry king. "Why is there no one here to attend me?" One of the men helping to dock his boat replied, "While you were hunting, I saw some walking on the road to Mengo!"

"Ah!" stormed the monarch in a rage. "They have gone to the white men. Am I no longer king here? Those white men burned down my palace, and now they are stealing my pages. Where is Mwafu?" At least I can count on him to bring his master a cool drink."

A servant replied, "Mwafu has gone with Denis to the priest's house to learn religion."

"What! Even Mwafu! Am I no longer king here? Have the white men taken over my country? No one obeys me any longer. My wants no longer matter even to the pages." He continued ranting along this theme until he arrived at his enclosure at the temporary palace. There he could be heard shouting over and over, "Mwafu! Mwafu! Come here!"

The small retinue of page boys present ran everywhere looking for the *Katakiro's* son, who was last seen returning along the road with Denis, a sixteen-year-old Catholic boy, who had been baptized the night after the martyrdom of Joseph Mukasa. In his new position as a baptized Christian, his fervor had reached even greater heights and he wished to bring everyone at court into the fold. With this end in mind, he had been teaching Mwafu the catechism, and, this particular morning, had taken him to Father Lourdel to tell him that Mwafu was now a catechumen.

Hearing the king shouting his name, Mwafu ran quickly to the inner chamber where the monarch grabbed him by the arm. "Where have you come from?" he demanded, shaking the frightened boy.

"I have been with Denis."

"What have you been doing?"

"He has been teaching me religion."

"Teaching you religion! Have I not forbidden the teaching of religion here? Am I no longer lord in my

78

own kingdom!" With this he grabbed a poison spear by the side of the throne and began striking Denis on the head and shoulders with it, until the young boy fell to the ground, covered with blood. "So you dare to disobey me," he shouted. "Here, take this wretch and kill him! I have had enough!"

Two of the guards dragged the unconscious Denis from the king's presence and left him in a pool of blood in one of the prison huts.

Meanwhile, not content to attack a Catholic, the raging Mwanga next rushed to the nearby storeroom, whose guardian was a prominent Anglican, Apollo Kagwa. Storming into the large hut, he shouted, "Are you a reader at the English mission?"

"Yes, I am," replied the young man with dignity.

"Then I shall teach you to read my way," roared the king breaking his spear in two and belaboring the Christian on the back and head with it. Then he kicked him over and over, threw Apollo's books into the fire and left with the warning, "Don't pray anymore!" This same Christian survived the massacre of the next few days, and was one of the leading sources of information about the martyrs. He later became a prime minister of Uganda.

Continuing his violent march through the palace, Mwanga ordered the castration of two of his subjects, one a Roman Catholic, James Buzabaliawo, a musician in the band, and a Protestant, Muddu-aguma, who both died shortly following the mutilation. Next he went to the house of the leader of the band, and one of his very favorites at court, Andrew Kaggwa. The king, not finding him there, vented his wrath on a leading Catholic, Honorat, the master of the household, whom he ordered thrown into prison and castrated.

Finally, tired from rushing about, Mwanga returned

to the throne room, where he ordered all the pages assembled at once. Then he ordered the gates to be closed and fires to be lit every few feet around the enclosure, so no Christians could escape.

Charles Lwanga, hearing the king's order, realized that the end might be near for all of them, so he called all of the pages and then had four of them stand at his side—Kizito, Mugagga, Gyavira and Mbaga. Addressing them in his most serious tone, yet lovingly, he began, "It appears that all of us may be called upon to witness to our faith at any moment. We may even be called upon to die for it, as have some of our friends this very day. As several of you have nearly finished your studies, and are quite ready to be baptized, I propose to do it myself, so you may go to your deaths bravely as full members of the church." Thus saying, he sent Kizito to fetch a bowl of water, and Mbaga to find a ladle. Then, with these at hand, he poured water over each one's head and baptized them. What names he gave them for their initiation into the Catholic church have not come down in any record.

"Now," he continued, "when the king calls for you to forsake your religion, you can boldly stand with me and say you are Catholics, and will never deny your faith." Then seeing that little Kizito was shaking all over with shock from the dreadful atrocities he had witnessed all day, Charles took his hand and reassuring him said, "Don't be afraid little one. When the moment comes for us to stand up for our religion, I shall be at your side all the time. If we have to die for Jesus, we shall die together, hand in hand."

Kizito smiled sweetly up at his hero. "Now I am not afraid, for I am a baptized Christian just like you." After months of fruitlessly importuning Father Lourdel, Kizito's dream at last had been realized.

80

CHAPTER SEVEN

CONDEMNED

While Mwanga had been running about shouting for his favorite boy, Mwafu, other pages were also missing, likewise for religious reasons.

Mubi had gone up to the English mission house where he was seated with a group on the veranda listening to the Reverend Mr. Ashe recount the Parable of the Seeds. Mubi wondered if he would prove to be good soil, where the seed of God's word could multiply and grow. Just as the group ended the lessons by singing the hymn, "All the people bow before Thee," Mr. Mackay arrived with the news that King Mwanga had given orders to seize all Christians.

Ashe and Mackay stopped singing immediately and thrust their students through a hole in the reed wall, where they escaped to their homes as fast as they could run. This was just in time, as the king's officer arrived a few minutes later.

Mubi was racing along a path to the nearby wooded hill, when he began to think of the seed. "If he ran away what sort of good soil would that be? Such action would only give the pagans reason for the repeated accusation that the Christians at court were insincere and just hoped to get material things from the missionaries. No. This he could not do.

Mubi slowed down, and turned his steps toward the palace at Munyonyo. On arrival he slipped in, and took his place with the other pages who were now assembled to go before the king.

Also true to their baptismal vows to "continue as Christ's faithful soldiers and servants unto their life's end" were three older Anglicans, who made no resistance or attempt to escape when the king's men came to put them in prison.

They were Noah Walukaga, a blacksmith, who insisted that his wife escape, but remained home quietly awaiting the executioners. Another Anglican was Robert Munyagabyanjo, the man who recovered Bishop Hannington's diary and brought it to the mission after paying for it himself. He was engaged in prayer with some boys when the executioners arrived. Pushing aside the reed wall of his house, he sent the youngsters fleeing to safety. Even though he had a gun handy, he asked nothing of his captors except a moment to put on his white robe before they led him away.

Still another, Alexander Kodoko, like Mubi, went to the court and turned himself in. All of these older men had been baptized, but poor Mubi, deemed too young and not properly prepared, had never received the sacrament.

Knowing the predicament of many of their followers, Mackay and Ashe attempted to see the king to prevail upon him to spare their people. When he refused, they sent out a letter to set their hearts at rest. It read:

People of God who are in Buganda, In days of old, Christians were hated, hunted and driven out and persecuted for Jesus' sake, and so it is today. Our beloved brethren, do not deny our Lord Jesus and He will not deny you on that great day when He shall come with glory. Do not cease to pray exceedingly, and to pray for our brethren who are in affliction, and those who do not know God.

Believers who are not yet baptized may be sure of salvation, if the omission did not arise from disobedience to God's commands.

May God deliver you out of all your afflictions! May He give you entrance into eternal life through Jesus Christ our Saviour,

We are your white brethren who have written to you.

Alexander Mackay
Rev. R.P. Ashe

Father Lourdel, likewise, made every attempt to save his Catholic pages from death. The French mission was at Mengo, eight miles away. The priest walked the distance through the thick red mud of the rain-washed road to the temporary palace. He sent a page in to request an audience with the king. But Mwanga was busy with his chiefs for whom he had sent earlier. Wanting the backing of his country's leaders in further persecution, he began another long harangue, "You are supposed to supply me with loyal servants, but you have given me nothing but traitors. Everyone who is bad in your clans you send to me. I have told them not to practice religion, but they no longer obey me. They have learned from the white men to rebel against me. What do you propose I do with them?"

All the chiefs, fearing the king's anger, abandoned their own sons, shouting, "Master, we are not to blame. Your pages have been put under a spell by the white men. Kill them all and we shall get you better ones."

"Very well. It is settled," said the *Kabaka*, and sent an order that all the court pages were to be assembled before him at once. Meanwhile, the cruel chiefs bowed down before him and thanked the king for not punishing them for the crimes of their children!

Father Lourdel kept pacing up and down outside the audience hall hoping that he would be called in to plead for his children. But time passed and he was still standing there, risking his life by coming to the court of the angry king. Mwanga refused to see him.

After a while, when all the pages were gathered together, Charles Lwanga, holding radiantly happy Kizito by the hand, led in the entire troop of about thirty, aged thirteen to twenty-five, to the audience hall where the king awaited them.

In the dim light of the huge thatched audience hall, the whites of the berserk king's eyes flashed sparks of anger, as he sat in judgment upon his throne. Behind and around him stood his chieftains in their long robes and tarbushes, looking grim and harsh. On the king's right was Mukajanga, chief executioner, already decked out in his ceremonial costume of grass wig, feathers and bells. Red clay was daubed all over his face. Gradually his assistants, dressed in animal skins and beating drums, joined the group. There were almost a hundred of them gathered like vultures awaiting the prey.

After they entered the hall, Charles led the way to the throne and prostrated himself before the *Kabaka*.

The entire group followed suit. When each had made his formal greeting, the king spoke, "Are all the pages here?" Assured that they were, he ordered the gates closed. Then pointing his finger at the crowd of young men and boys, many of whom had been destined to be leaders of their country, Mwanga shouted, "All those who practice the white men's religion, go over there to the wall. Those who do not pray, stay here near me."

Charles Lwanga stood apart at once, saying, "There is no denying that which a man knows to be true." He grabbed Kizito by the hand, stepped over to the wall, and was followed immediately by all the Christian pages, both Catholic and Protestant.

Only a few remained by the king's side. He was obviously disappointed and even more infuriated. "Is there no one here but my dog who will bother to obey me? Just this handful remain true to me." Then, looking closely at the small group who had remained, he continued, "Are you sure that none among you pray?"

"None, sire," they replied. Still not convinced, he walked closer to them. Pointing to a trembling boy, he screamed, "Wasswa, you are a liar. I have seen you go many times to the English mission. You are one who prays. Go and join the other traitors."

Wasswa stumbled over to the Christian group, all of whom looked ashamed to be anywhere near him. Only Mubi held out his hand, and said, "Come, dear friend, do not be afraid to die for Jesus. We shall all go to heaven together. Rather, rejoice." The twenty-three Christian pages waited together almost joyfully for the king to speak again, happy to declare their faith.

Once more he demanded, "Are all of you Christians?"

"Yes, we are," they stated most emphatically.

"Do you still want to remain Christians?"

"Yes, and that we shall remain."

"You see," shrieked the monarch, lurching about on his throne, "how your children have rebelled against me."

"Kill them! Kill them!" shouted all the assembled chiefs. "We shall give you others!"

Then the cruel king passed the sentence which eventually threw these obscure African youngsters into worldwide prominence, and gave them an exalted place in heaven as canonized saints. "Seize all these who pray. Take them to Namugongo and burn them alive. I, Mwanga, have spoken."

Of the thirteen execution sites, Namugongo was the one reserved for chiefs and royalty. It was located fourteen miles from Munyonyo.

At Mwanga's word, the executioners pounced upon their victims. They beat them to the ground and began tying them up with ropes about their hands and necks. While they were busy attending to this, the king noticed his favorite, Mwafu, son of the prime minister, among the group of youngest pages. Pointing at the light-skinned boy, who had only just started on the road to Christianity, but who now had bravely stepped apart to join the group professing Christ, he said, "Release that one, and put him in the stocks for four days. He shall not die."

Then Mukajanga sidled up to the king and whispered something in his ear. It was to ask also a reprieve for his own son, Mbaga, only sixteen, one of the boys baptized that morning by Charles Lwanga. The king nodded his head in approval, not wanting to offend a man of such dread importance.

Mukajanga then went over to the group of youngest pages, roped together like a bundle of hay, and said,

"Son, only say that you have given up praying, and I will get your release."

The boy shook his head emphatically. "No, I am a Christian and wish to die with my friends."

Mukajanga was not one to give up easily. He sent his chief assistant, Sebatta, to make another attempt. "Since when have you been a Christian? Your father bids you run away quickly. I will release your bonds!"

But the brave young Catholic stood staunchly up to his tormentor. "My real Father, whom I must obey above all, is in heaven. Leave me alone. I am truly a Christian as I have said."

Other Christians who had been in the prison overnight, were next brought to the courtyard. The entire group was sent off to begin their tortuous journey to the distant execution site. Kizito, tied tightly to the other youngest pages, laughed merrily as they tried to walk in their clumsy bonds. "We look like a bug with a thousand feet! Isn't this crazy, trying to walk all jumbled together!"

Wasswa didn't think it quite so funny as he was in the middle of the tightly squeezed mob and could hardly breathe.

Father Lourdel was still waiting in the outer court, hoping for an audience with the blood-maddened king. He saw his beloved converts pass by on their way to death for professing the religion he had taught them. His heart was nearly breaking, but he was utterly unable to help them. The priest raised his hand in greeting and made the sign of the cross in the air as they passed.

The group of Protestant pages, under the care of Moses Mukasa, who was in charge of the outer court, had also made their profession of faith, and were thrown together with the Catholic group under

Charles Lwanga. The two head pages had met earlier that day just before the groups were brought before the irate monarch. Charles informed Moses that he had just baptized several of his younger pages who had been under instruction for a year.

Moses had not been authorized to perform baptisms, and thus did not follow suit. He still expected to hear from the Reverend Mr. Ashe, in some way, just what he should do. Meanwhile he had exhorted his boys as they clustered around him for news of their fate. "We also are going to be killed. But do not renounce your religion. Let us pray for courage!" This they did, kneeling together on the hard mud floor of the court. It was in this way that two close friends left on their journey to martyrdom—Kizito a baptized Catholic, but Mubi still just an Anglican catechumen. He had hoped to be washed of his sins. But instead, they were to be burned away with fire at Namugongo.

Friendship between the two groups of catechumens, Catholics and Anglicans, had always been maintained on a high level. As James Miti, the Ugandan historian of the martyrs, wrote, "During the persecution there was never a distinction of religion or denomination; we were all Christians, whether one went to Mackay or Pere Lourdel for religious instruction. All Christian converts were one family, with two internal arbitrary divisions. We loved one another and wished one another well."

Catholics harbored Anglicans and vice versa during the horrible days before and after Namugongo. It was through mutual help that many survived to pick up the traces and start again the work of God's kingdom in Uganda.

Now the prisoners were jumbled together, regardless of denomination, joined side to side by the ropes and their all-consuming faith in Jesus Christ. They prayed not that they would be delivered from their fate; but that they would remain true to their Lord in the hour of martyrdom.

Added to this group of pages at court, were two soldiers, Bruno and Pontian, both Catholics; Andrew Kaggwa, leader of the Catholics at Kigowa; and two Anglicans, Nasibu, the king's tailor, and Byatunga, keeper of the royal hearth. Altogether the party of condemned Christians totaled thirty-two, as they waited at Munyonyo to begin their long journey to Namugongo.

That afternoon, the cruel chancellor learned that his hated enemy, Andrew Kaggwa, the king's chief drummer, was among the prisoners. He called for Kaggwa to be brought before him.

"Was it you that taught my children religion and have caused my own son, Mwafu, to turn against me?"

"Yes, it was I," replied the thirty-year-old Christian leader and catechist. "What of it? Have I taught them the plague?"

"Yes, you have taught them the plague. They are as good as dead!"

The Moslem chancellor took this opportunity to call the chief executioner to his side. "Take this man and kill him. I will not eat again until you bring me his arm!"

The chief and eight executioners dressed in animal skins and shrieking like banshees surrounded the martyr robed only in a loin cloth and bark cloth toga. They took him to a thicket back of the chancellor's residence where they threw him to the ground and cut off his arm at the shoulder. In his remaining hand, Andrew clutched a small prayer book. The only sound which could be heard from him was a continual murmur, "My God! My God!" Finally they cut off his head and hacked his corpse to pieces.

A few minutes later one of the chancellor's men returned to the *Katakiro* carrying the bleeding arm, suspended from a length of fiber. The remaining pieces of the brave martyr were left for the vultures to pick clean.

All day the group of prisoners had been quartered in the courtyard. Then, at five o'clock, the fatal march began. The Christians, tethered together by ropes around their necks, walked the red dust path to Dengo in single file.

The executioners played upon their drums and jangled their bells to warn all on the road that death was on the march. It was customary, however, to kill one of the victims as they started on their grim journey. The king's guard, Pontian, said, "Kill me here. I have told you I am a Christian. Why should I walk all the way to Namugongo to die?"

With that the chief executioner obliged by driving his spear into the martyr's chest. When Pontian did not die immediately, he plunged it a second time into his neck. This time the valiant Catholic was finished. "Cut off his head," shouted Mukajanga, who had just remarked that Pontian's flesh was as soft as butter. Then the frightened boys thus began their march through the pools of blood of their fellow martyr.

Three hours later, at dusk, they reached Mengo, the site of the burned-out palace of the king. Here it was decided to rest for the night. The guards and executioners marched the prisoners off in pairs to be put in wooden stocks so they could not escape. Mukajanga, the head executioner, grabbed Kizito and Mubi by their necks and threw them together.

"You little ones are about the same size. You can

entertain each other in the stocks."

With that he held out a wooden beam having in it four holes for arms, and gestured to the boys to stretch out their hands and slip them through the holes. Then wooden sticks were put alongside their wrists so the hands could not be withdrawn. Iron shackles were put on their feet.

"How do we eat with these things on?" asked Mubi, whose small black body was aching all over with hunger and fatigue.

Looking longingly towards Charles Lwanga, shackled amid a group of other young Catholics, Kizito replied, "I don't care about eating, but I wish I could be over there with Master Charles. They are all praying together." It was evening and they were reciting the Angelus.

"Come now, Kizito, don't be like that," begged Mubi. "If you and I can die together for Christ, why can't we pray together?"

"I suppose we can," replied Kizito, sniffling a bit, but having no hands free to wipe his eyes or nose. "Do you know how to say the Hail Mary?"

"No. I don't. But I'll learn it. How does it go?"

Kizito began, "Hail Mary, full of grace . . ." while Mubi listened carefully and tried to repeat it.

Then Mubi asked Kizito if he could say the 23rd Psalm

"What's that?" asked Kizito, twisting his head in puzzlement.

"Listen. It goes like this. The Lord is my shepherd, I shall not want. . . ."

When he had finished, Kizito said, "That was very beautiful, and comforting, too. But I just thought of something you surely must know, the Our Father.

"Why, yes! That is what we call the Lord's Prayer.

Let us say it together now." In the distance could be heard the murmur of the Catholic pages saying the Rosary, and the Anglican pages reciting evensong.

Kizito finished the prayer and looked up. Mubi still had his eyes closed and was saying, "for thine is the kingdom . . . for ever and ever," when he stopped and asked, "Kizito, why don't you finish the prayer? Why stop in the middle?"

"Stop in the middle?" replied Kizito. "That's all there is."

"No it isn't. Mr. Ashe taught us to finish with the words, "For thine is the kingdom, and the power and the glory, for ever and ever. Amen.""

"Well, Father Lourdel didn't. He said it ended with "deliver us from evil.""

"This is a sorry way for us to be acting when we are so near to death and heaven," said Mubi. "I will end where you do."

"Oh no," cried Kizito. "I will learn it your way."

Then in the midst of their pain and hunger, the two boys let out peals of laughter, so that the puzzled executioners turned to stare in amazement. They wondered how, in such a hopeless state, these Christian pages could even smile, and yet their hearts were filled with joy and laughter!

CHAPTER EIGHT

THE ROAD
TO NAMUGONGO

The next morning the boys awoke in the early mist of dawn, their thin black limbs shaking with the cold. Although Uganda is on the equator, it is four thousand feet above sea level, and consequently very cold at night. No covering had been given the prisoners and they had been required to sleep on the cold ground of the former palace in Mengo. Neither had anything been given them to eat or drink.

The guards came around and loosened their shackles, offering them steamed bananas for breakfast. As soon as their hands were released from the stocks, the prisoners knelt to say their morning prayers. When finished, Kizito remarked, "What a night, Mubi, you do not make the best bedfellow!"

"I ache all over and it is because you pulled me this way and that," said Mubi.

"I pulled? Look at my wrists, rubbed raw from you

pulling the stock in *your* direction."

"This is no way to begin our last day, Kizito. Here, let's eat while our hands are free."

In a corner nearby, bound together for the night, were Wasswa and Mbaga. Everyone was watching the strange scene taking place over there. Mukajanga had released the boys from their stocks and was trying to drag Mbaga away. "Come now, son, I will take you home with me. Your mother and sisters will be able to persuade you to give up this foolishness. You are not a Christian. Why should you die?"

"I am! I am!" cried Mbaga, pulling back toward Wasswa. "Why don't you take *him*? He doesn't want to die. He even denied his faith."

Wasswa drew back in shame and horror. "Oh no, it is not true. I have changed my mind. Now I am glad to die for Christ, my Savior. Please don't say that again." Wasswa's shoulders shook with grief at the memory of his cowardice.

"I will not listen to anything further. You are coming with me." With that, Mukajanga dragged off the struggling would-be martyr.

As it turned out, the execution of the prisoners was not to take place for another eight days. Mukajanga was sure that a week at home, with all his relatives imploring him, would surely sway his young son from his deadly course. But, he did not appreciate the strength of conviction of the young Catholic convert fresh from his recent baptism.

However, Kizito was not convinced. He said quite loudly, "I bet he will deny his religion."

Charles Lwanga would hear no such talk and scolded, "No, he will not. I think they are only tempting him again. Let us all pray that he holds fast to the end."

While the executioners were preparing their prisoners for the daylong march from Mengo to Namugongo, two other Christians who were working there rebuilding the palace, turned themselves in to their chief. They did this rather than endanger their friends and companions, who had been harboring them. These two were Mathias Kalemba and Luke Banabakintu, both staunch older Catholics who had been baptized years before. They had served as spiritual leaders of their communities during the temporary withdrawal from Uganda of the French priests.

Having kept these two overnight in stocks and painful slave yokes, their chief then turned them over to the Moslem chancellor who had been sent to Mengo to try Christians.

Hailed before the *Katakiro,* white-haired Mathias, the oldest of the martyrs, was questioned about his faith.

"I hear," said the Mohammedan, "that you have but one wife, and have sent away the others. I suppose you cook your own food now?"

"Have I been brought before you because I am thin, or because of my religion?" countered Mathias.

"Why do you pray? What would induce a man of your age and position to adopt the white man's religion?"

"I follow that religion because I want to," replied the dauntless Catholic leader from Ssingo.

Then the accuser turned to Luke and asked if he also pleaded guilty to the charge of being a Christian. To this he replied, "Yes, I do."

"Then," said the chancellor, "I condemn you both to be burned alive." As the brave men were being led away, Mukasa added, "And see that Mathias Kalemba suffers a greater torture, since he is a leader of the Christians."

The executioners were only too happy to oblige and rushed off with their prisoners towards the road to Namugongo. When they had only traveled ten minutes of the long journey, Mathias announced that he would go no further. "What is the use of walking all the way to Namugongo? Kill me here!"

Remembering the parting words of their chancellor to make Mathias suffer long, the executioners set to work applying all the refinements of their cruel trade. First they cut off his hands and feet, then chopped away his arms at his elbows and his legs at his knees. Then to make certain that he did not die immediately from loss of blood, they sutured his veins and arteries with fiber. The valiant martyr never uttered a cry or murmur against his tormentors, but only called out to his fellow Catholic, "Luke, we shall meet again in heaven."

Angered by his strength and courage in not begging for mercy, the torturers next cut slivers of flesh from Mathias' back. Making a fire, they roasted his own body before his eyes. Then, finally tiring of their sport, they departed with Luke and left what remained of the limbless martyr on the bloodied path.

Here he lay for three horrible days, attacked by flies and hungry black ants, in the sweltering African sun. Some men, coming down the path, stumbled upon him. Horrified by the inhuman sight before them, they ran quickly from the spot, but not before they heard him cry out, as had his dying Master long ago, "I thirst."

Not until May 30th did the valiant sufferer find relief from his prolonged agony. Mathias died alone, uncomforted and unattended on the road to

Namugongo. A memorial now marks the spot of his martyrdom, but for him there was no grave. The vultures and hyenas carried off the dismembered remains.

His companion, Luke, was hurried along to catch up with the other prisoners.

Kizito, Mubi and all the other Christian pages from the court of Mwanga were once again strung neck to neck in a long line and marched the remaining seven miles to the royal execution site. On the way, their young eyes were to view horror and bloodshed again and again. The guards had been unable to remove the iron shackles from twenty-year-old Gonzaga, and he was forced to march with the cumbersome irons rubbing and cutting into his swollen ankles.

He tried to keep up with the rest of the party, but his chains held him back. The guards hit him and pressed him onwards, but, with the blood running down over his feet which were covered with flies and pus, he just could not keep up. Finally, Mukajanga, annoyed with the delay, plunged a spear into the heart of the faltering young page. Left where he had fallen, the sight of his pierced body added to the trauma of his former companions. Yet they never lost their courage but continued to pray as they marched, several of them leading the others in hymns.

At last the sordid journey came to an end. The party of martyrs arrived at the chosen site of their fiery execution. But if they thought their sufferings were soon to be over, they were greatly mistaken. Eight more days of continued pain and wretchedness lay before them.

Here they were lodged by twos and threes in the grass huts of their executioners. But they were allowed no freedom. Some had their necks locked in iron collars attached to the supporting poles of the huts. Others were in neck yokes, and still more in stocks on both their hands and their feet.

They were given very little food and no coverings for the cold nights. Yet somehow during this long week of imprisonment, all were able to keep up their spirits, and continued to say their daily prayers. The boys began to find and use liturgical forms common to both the Anglican and Catholic traditions—like the Creed and the Lord's Prayer. The walls between them disappeared under the stress of persecution.

As soon as the missionaries learned that all the prisoners had not been killed immediately, but were being held at Namugongo, they hurried to do everything possible to procure their release.

On May 29th, Mr. Mackay went to the palace and reminded the king, "You promised me a short while ago that you would give me anything I liked if I would show your gunsmith how to make cartridge cases. I did it and now I ask my reward. Will you give it?"

Mwanga, whose chief practical interest lay in guns and munitions, replied, "Yes."

"Then I beg you for the lives of my condemned Christians, those whom you have not yet executed."

"If any remain alive, I promise I will not kill them," answered the wily king.

Mackay, however, was unimpressed, and added, "Let the executioner be brought in. Tell him you countermand your previous orders."

Mwanga refused, nor would he command a messenger to go to the executioner. "I have already given orders to spare some. All the rest are dead." This was true in part, because three young pages were released unharmed five days later just before the others were executed.

Mackay felt it unsafe to press the king further. Mwanga was showing signs of irritation, and might in a fit of anger order further executions.

For much the same reason, Father Lourdel felt it wisest not to go with Mackay when he suggested they appear together at court.

During this very week of fearsome events, Father Livinhac, who had gone to France to be consecrated bishop of Eastern Equatorial Africa, arrived in Rubaga on May 27th. Mackay immediately dispatched a note to him suggesting that the Anglican and Catholic missionaries go together to Mwanga. Perhaps their combined numbers would force the king to stay the execution.

Bishop Livinhac politely declined, explaining that his opinion, based on his prior experience in Uganda, was that such a joint effort would more than likely spur Mwanga on to further atrocities.

The new bishop, however, just two days before the holocaust, went to pay his respects to Mwanga in company with Fathers Lourdel and Denoit. He brought gifts in payment for his fare across Lake Victoria in the royal canoes. He found the young king very changed from their last confrontation three years earlier. Mwanga was now dissipated, his face drawn, his speech incoherent. Bishop Livinhac told him, as diplomatically as possible, that he was destroying the future of his own people by the persecution of outstanding Christians. He threatened to withdraw his mission from the country unless the unbearable situation came to a halt.

Alexander Mackay had also asked that the English mission be allowed to leave. Ashe was given permission to depart, but Mr. Mackay was held a virtual prisoner as he reported in a letter home to his father. "Again I have sorrowful news to tell, even more distressing than before. Only a month ago violent persecution against the Christians broke out, and they have been murdered right and left. . . . Those in the palace grounds, and the more conspicuous and well-known Christians, were first seized. About a dozen were hacked to pieces the first day, and their members left lying in all directions on the road. . . . As in the case of Bishop Hannington, we were helpless, and expected every moment our own arrest. . . .

"Nearly all our best friends [were] arrested suddenly, and murdered almost before our very eyes. . . . We ourselves, too, are in a position of the gravest danger. This tyrant is rash and vain, and fancies that there is no power in the world that can call his vilest and most cruel acts in question. . . . He has given out that he means to hold us as hostages, fearing that the white men will be upon him for murder of the bishop with his fifty porters, besides all his other cruelties."

During these futile entreaties, preparations for the martyrs' conflagration continued throughout the week. A low platform was constructed of tree limbs at the foot of Namugongo hill. Firewood was collected and piled up nearby for the pyre. Reeds were cut and woven together for mats in which the martyrs were each to be wrapped before being placed on the platform.

During all these gruesome preparations, the intended victims continued to maintain their cheerful attitude. They were thrilled and happy to be able to die for their faith. This unusual situation appalled the executioners, who were accustomed to continual importunings for mercy and deliverance by their victims.

Kizito and Mubi, from their distant prison in the guard's hut, could sometimes see and hear the activities of their executioners. The stagnant days seemed endlessly long to the boys who were accustomed to constant activity and daily sports such as swimming and wrestling. Here there was nothing to do but contemplate their gruesome fate.

The night of June 2nd was a sleepless one for prisoners and jailers alike. The hundred or so executioners spent the midnight hours preparing for the morrow's execution by leaping about in their regalia of feathers, paint and grass. The moonlit air was rent hideously with their antiphonal shrieks and chants. To perform such a ceremonial act of torture and horror, the perpetrators would need to be somewhat out of their minds.

Plantain wine added to their intoxication, as they whirled about madly in a frenzied dance of death.

As the sun rose, and a cold mist lifted from the ground, the painted executioners came for their victims. None of the prisoners had been able to sleep during the continued beating of drums and ritual shrieks and howls. They had spent most of the night in prayer.

In between recitations of the Lord's Prayer and memorizing each other's favorite devotions, Kizito and Mubi had occasionally discussed their death sentence.

"Do you think we will die right away? asked Mubi, "or will it take a long time?"

"How would I know? I have not been burned alive before. But I hope the smoke will kill us before the fire does. That is what happened to many victims of the palace fire. Remember?"

Mubi pulled at the iron ring which had rubbed his

neck raw. "Well, at least today we will escape from *these* things."

Kizito looked at Mubi and wondered, "Do I look that awful?" Their curly hair and dark bodies were covered with dirt and dust. Their faces were sunken and drawn from lack of food and sleep. On their wrists and ankles were numerous pus-filled sores caused by the stocks. But at the same time he remarked to Mubi, "You know, I really do not mind suffering when it is for Christ. It will all be over soon, perhaps in an hour, and then we will be in heaven with Jesus and the saints."

Mubi looked downcast. "I wish I could be so sure. I have not even been baptized."

"Mubi, what a foolish thought! Of course you will go to heaven. You are giving your life for your faith. What could be more glorious?!"

Just then the shadow of a hideous apparition crossed the doorway to the hut. It was Mukajanga in full ceremonial regalia holding his son, Mgaba, by the hand. He threw the boy on the filthy mud floor and wiped his hands on his leopard skin. "Die, if you want! I give up."

"Mbaga Tuzinde! Mbaga! We thought you had left!" shouted Mubi and Kizito in chorus.

"No, no. I have been all week at the plantation of my father, where all of my relatives have begged me to give up Christianity. They pleaded and bribed, but I refused. My father finally realized that I meant it and has brought me here to die with you."

"God be praised," said little Kizito, who had been among those praying that Mbaga would not recant.

Then there was a deadly silence for a few minutes, followed by the steady beat of a ceremonial drum. The official start of the execution had been sounded.

CHAPTER NINE

THE BURNING
AT NAMUGONGO

All the prisoners were gathered in the small square
in front of Mukajanga's hut. Lined up again, the
younger boys strung together with neck halters, they
set off for the pyre. A hundred guards danced about
them wildly singing and chanting of the offering of
human lives which they were going to make to their
gods.

Faces covered with ochre and ashes, the
executioners were a terrifying sight as they whirled
about in animal skins, the amulets about their necks
and waists, clinking, and gongs and cymbals clashing.
Throughout the mile-long march they shrieked at
their victims, "The women who have born you shall
weep today. You have offended our gods, Nende,
Mukasa and Kibuka. For this you must die."

In contrast to this scene of pagan madness, the
Christians represented a calm and joyous sight as they

greeted one another with cries of delight and encouragement to remain firm in their faith to the end. Kizito and Mubi and several other of the younger pages who were tied together prayed continually as they marched, and tried not to think of the fire, but rather their reception into heaven.

The group of thirty-two victims was led a long way around the River Lukingiridder. According to custom, no prisoner could be executed who had passed through its waters. As they walked single file down the side of the hill toward the pyre arranged at its foot, they were met by Senkole, guardian of the sacred fire. As each martyr passed by, Senkole struck him lightly on the head with his torch and intoned, "Your own disobedience is responsible for your death, and not the *Kabaka*." But three he did not tap. They were the very young pages, Charles Werabe, Simeon Sebuta, and Denis Kamyuka who was later, in 1920, the chief witness at the beatification process. Although Kizito was even younger than they, he nevertheless received a ceremonial tap from Senkole's torch. For him there was no reprieve.

But the boys released from death were heartbroken. "We had hoped to die together," they wept. Trying to console them, their fellow Catholic, Bruno Serunkuma, former guardian of the king's armory, said, "I am sorry for you. It is clear that the king has pardoned you but only because he wants you to give up your religion. Keep the faith."

And Muggagga, himself only sixteen, added, "My poor Kamyuka, you are going to miss the rendezvous in heaven."

But Senkole now had another tradition to fulfill. As guardian of the sacred fire, he was not supposed to attend the actual execution. Instead, he had the privilege of reserving one of the victims on which to expend his personal talents. For this he chose the outstanding Catholic leader of the pages of the inner court, Charles Lwanga. Tapping the muscular twenty-five-year-old man on the shoulder, he now singled him out and led him a few yards apart. "You, I am keeping for myself to sacrifice to Kibuka, Mukasa and Nende. You will make a prime offering."

Charles called goodbye to his special friends, and gave a blessing to the young pages whom he had so recently baptized with his own hand. Seeing his mentor and friend being led away, Kizito cried out, "Charles, Charles!"

The kindly young man, realizing the fear in Kizito's young heart at losing his friend right at the most dreaded moment said, "Do not weep for me, Kizito. Goodbye, we shall soon all meet in heaven."

"That is true," called back the boy wiping away his tears and smiling. "In a very little while we shall all see Jesus Christ!"

The large party passed on and Charles was led alone to a nearby tree by his executioner, Senkole and an assistant, Sebabi. Here a smaller pyre had been arranged. Charles was tied up tightly with his arms fastened to his side, both feet held firmly in an extended position. His body was attached to the tree with fiber ropes and his legs and feet placed over the fagots. While this was being done, Charles told his torturers how happy he would be if they would embrace his religion. Then the cruel Senkole lit a handful of grass from the sacred torch and set fire to the wood under the martyr's feet.

As the flames mounted Charles began to sweat profusely and, breathing heavily, saw that it would be very long before he would die. He never lost consciousness as the intense heat seared away the flesh from his feet and then burned through the bones.

All the while his tormentor threw taunts in his face, "Let us see whether your God will come to deliver you from the fire! See you are now punished properly for your disloyalty."

But without a cry of pain or anger, the suffering martyr spoke back, "You poor, foolish man. It seems to me that you are pouring cool water over my feet. But be forewarned. I am dying for my religion but someday you will burn forever in a permanent fire, the fire of hell."

At this point the flames rose higher and Charles spoke no more, but lay in agony praying to the last. Suddenly above the roar of the fire his torturers heard him cry, "My God." Finally, his spirit was released from the charred body and ascended into heaven—on the very anniversary of the Ascension of his Lord.

As soon as the fire had completely consumed the martyr, Senkole and his assistant took handfuls of young reeds and buds. Strewing them about the foot of the tree, they chanted, "It is not we who have killed you, but Nende and Kibuka and all the gods whom you have despised."

Meanwhile the remainder of the large party of thirty-one victims and a hundred executioners had at last arrived at the funeral pyre. It was thirty feet long and twenty-one feet wide, built as a wooden scaffold about three feet above the ground. Underneath were branches and fagots of all sizes piled thickly. At intervals along the sides were bunches of grass and additional quantities of firewood.

The martyrs had been stripped of their white robes before leaving the court and dressed in ragged bark cloth. This was now removed from them and hung upon a tree. Standing there in embarrassment with nothing on but small loin cloths, Kizito remarked, "It does not matter. In a short time we shall be clothed in the nuptial garment which will admit us to the heavenly banquet." Then they all sat down in a group. Mukajanga gave them each a gourdful of banana wine which was the custom before an execution, but James Buzabaliawo refused the drink just as Jesus had before His crucifixion.

By then it was high noon with the hot sun directly overhead. The executioners laid the reed mats on the ground and, tying each martyr's feet and arms tightly with fiber ropes, rolled them up in the mats. It was impossible to move, but the brave Christians could still speak.

Kizito called out to Mukajanga, "You big devil, you will burn like the tobacco in your pipe, you dealer in sorcery." The head executioner then rushed over to Kizito and threw him on the readied pyre shouting, "Who is going to burn now?"

Next Mubi was lifted up and laid beside Kizito, then the other youngest pages, Muggaga, Gyavira and Wasswa. All were tied tightly in their reed shrouds awaiting the last moment of the pagan rite. Kizito called out, "Let's say the Our Father and suffer bravely."

The three boys who had been granted reprieve were also trussed and rolled up in mats. But they were set aside, not on the execution platform. They protested loudly, "We are Christians, too, and we shall never abandon our religion. Burn us too!"

But Mukajanga didn't have time to bother with them, for he had suddenly realized—with horror—that his own son, Mbaga, had been wrapped in a reed mat and, like his comrades, was lying on the platform awaiting execution. Overcome with grief, the chief executioner ordered his son removed. The other boys watched as Mbaga was unwrapped and led away under a tree. There he knelt before his father and begged that he not spare him. Mukajanga motioned to one of his assistants who took the boy aside and struck him dead with a club on the back of the head. Immediately Mbaga's body was carried back by his heartbroken father and laid on the pyre.

Three others, each of them highly placed at court, were likewise given the *coup de grace* before the fire was ignited. But Robert Munyagabyanjo, the Anglican council member who had secured Bishop Hannington's diary and given it to Mackay, was dismembered with an axe before his tormented torso was thrown on the pyre.

Everything was now in readiness. More wood was thrown on top of the victims, and the wildly prancing executioners lit their torches from the sacred fuse. At last, taking their places around the mammoth funeral pyre, they touched the fagots to the tinder. Kizito called out pitifully to the three children who had been released and were weeping with grief and horror, "Goodbye friends, we are on our way. We shall meet in heaven."

Meanwhile the hideous executioners had begun to leap into the air, brandishing their spears and screaming imprecations at their suffering victims. Mubi closed his eyes and tried to recall the story of the three children in the fiery furnace from the book of Daniel. Mr. Mackay had told his class the story soon after the first three Anglican boys had been burned alive. Mubi recalled that the words these Hebrew youths had said in prayer during their ordeal were the very same words they sang in chapel each Sunday during Morning Prayer. Mubi tried to recall them as the smoke began to roll over the upturned faces of the men and boys laid on their bed of fire.

He heard the snapping and crackling of the dry kindling as it caught fire. Then the whoosh and roar of the larger fagots as they ignited. The heat increased. Mubi suddenly felt terribly dizzy and thirsty. All around him he heard the soft praying voices of his companions and above them the banshee screams of the executioners. If only he could remember the prayer. Oh yes, it came with a rush just as the fire began to reach his reed casing and burn his frail dark body. Suddenly, above the roar of the fire could be heard the sweet young voice of Mubi as he prayed in his own fiery furnace, "Blessed art thou, O Lord God of our fathers: praised and exalted above all for ever.

"Blessed art thou for the Name of thy Majesty: praised and exalted above all for ever."

As the swirling flames of the raging inferno finally engulfed him, Mubi saw the sky open. Jesus came on a cloud of glory to take him to everlasting joy in heaven. With his last breath the little page boy exclaimed, "Blessed art thou on the glorious throne of thy kingdom!"

Kizito lying beside him had been reciting the Rosary. Even though his hands were not free to finger the beads, he had had much practice in remembering where he was in the prayers during his week in the constricting stocks. Although he was unable to move, Kizito was conscious that nowhere in that large group of suffering martyrs was there a sound of reproach or a cry of anguish. As he had quietly awaited the moment when the executioners would ignite the pyre, he realized that they had made the right decision. If Christianity is worth living for, then likewise, it must be worth dying for. It was not something you could take on lightly for political or material gain. To be a member with Christ, one must be willing to die with Christ, even if it means a death of torture.

Kizito felt proud and happy to be numbered among such brave men and boys who were literally laying down their lives on this massive funeral pyre.

As Mukajanga held the ceremonial torch to the fagots, he once more reproached the Christians, mocking them in the extra anguish he felt at the loss of his son. "You are to be roasted alive. Now we shall see if the God in whom you trust will come to deliver you."

Kizito called out bravely, "You can burn our bodies, but our souls you cannot touch. They will go to paradise." Following these words he closed his eyes and continued praying. The flames leapt around him and his companions began writhing in agony. As the roaring inferno engulfed the small boy, he heard a voice and opened his eyes.

Standing on top of the dancing flames was a vision of Jesus Christ in His shining resurrection robe. The Son of God held out his hand to the brave young saint, and called, "Come, Kizito, enter into the joy of thy Lord."

And Kizito, raising his head, cried out, "My Lord and my God." Then he fell back dead upon the fiercely burning mat.

The fire continued to rage in a huge red and orange inferno. Each time it showed the slightest inclination to die down, the executioners warily approached the dreadful heat and threw more branches on the conflagration. They also took great sticks and stoked the charred torsos and limbs deeper into the hottest part of the fire so nothing would later remain of the victims except ashes.

The three young would-be martyrs were kept at the site throughout the burning to assure that the sufferings of their friends would have a strong effect upon them so they would renounce their faith. As it turned out they were kept in prison a whole year afterwards. On release, only one, Sebuta, recanted.

But the effect of the martyrs' courage in the holocaust of Namugongo was most felt by the executioner's themselves. "We have put many people to death," they said, "but never such as these." On returning to court to report to King Mwanga, Mukajanga extolled them. "I have never executed people who showed such fortitude and courage and endurance. We never heard them cry out once, but they prayed aloud to God even in the flames. There was not even a moan or an angry word. They prayed until they died. Even the youngest, Kizito."

Henry M. Stanley, the famed explorer who first appealed to England for missionaries to come to Uganda, is shown here in an engraving made in the same year as the holocaust at Namugongo.

A woodcut of Stanley's ceremonious arrival on the shores of Mutesa's kingdom.

Mutesa's court, as Stanley found it.

Alexander Mackay was among the earliest to respond to Stanley's call in 1876. He was an engineer and the son of a Scottish clergyman.

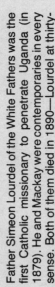

Father Simeon Lourdel of the White Fathers was the first Catholic missionary to penetrate Uganda (in 1879). He and Mackay were contemporaries in every sense. Both of them died in 1890—Lourdel at thirty-seven and Mackay at forty.

This is Mwanga who succeeded Mutesa as king and who was the perpetrator of the massacre of Christians at Namugongo and elsewhere.

White Fathers Magazine.

James Hannington was sent to Uganda in 1885 as the first Anglican bishop of equatorial Africa. He was slain, however, by Mwanga's men before he ever reached his destination.

Rubaga, capital of Mutesa's kingdom as it appeared in 1875, the same year that Stanley arrived there.

Today this Roman Catholic cathedral stands atop the very same hill in Rubaga that once housed Mutesa's government.

This is a section of Stanley's map of central Africa which was issued with the first edition of his two-volume book, *In Darkest Africa*, in 1890.

This building, here seen under construction, is the Mission of Our Lady of Kamoga which the White Fathers and their converts built south of Lake Victoria during their exile from Uganda in 1883-1884.

White Fathers and ransomed orphans at Our Lady of Kamoga, around 1885.

This royal tomb at Kasubi is an exact reproduction of the royal residence to which the missionaries came so often to implore the clemency of the king on behalf of the Christians.

White Fathers Magazine

This is the tomb of Andrew Kaggwa who was beheaded and hacked to pieces at Munyonyo on May 26, 1886.

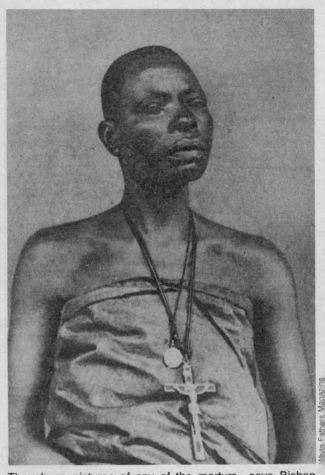

Though no pictures of any of the martyrs—save Bishop Hannington—have come down to us, this is Marie Mathilda, the sister of Noe Mawaggali who was speared and savaged by mad dogs at Mityana on the same day as the holocaust, June 3, 1886. After his gruesome death, she devoted herself to the work of the Catholic mission until her own death.

Young King Chua and his mother. Chua was proclaimed king of Buganda in August, 1897, after his father, Mwanga, had been deposed. At the time of his accession to the throne he was only a few months old.

On October 18, 1964, Pope Paul VI announced the canonization of the martyrs of Uganda. An excerpt from his speech, in which he also acknowledged the faithfulness of the Protestant martyrs, is printed in the back of this book as an appendix.

This is the church built on the site of the excruciating execution of Charles Lwanga at Namugongo, June 3, 1886.

A view of burgeoning Kampala taken in 1957.

A street scene in modern Kampala. The old-style pioneer buildings, like the one in the foreground, are rapidly being replaced by reinforced concrete structures like the one in the background.

A house in rural Uganda where peasant farmers subsist largely on a diet of bananas and other fresh fruits and vegetables. Famine is almost unknown in this lush country.

President Idi Amin, uncharacteristically out of uniform, is seen here at a press conference in October, 1976.

Religious News Service Photo

Archbishop Janani Luwum, who now takes his place in the ever-growing role of the martyrs of Uganda.

CHAPTER TEN

THE BLOOD OF THE MARTYRS IS THE SEED OF THE CHURCH

The Roman Catholic and Anglican martyrs of Uganda did not die in vain. Only four years after the June 3rd holocaust, there were already 12,000 Catholics in Uganda and an equal number of Anglicans. But this startling expansion was not made without the sacrifice of many white missionaries, who gave their lives as freely and lovingly as had the twenty-five black Christians at Namugongo.

Father Lourdel was only thirty-seven when one of Africa's fatal fevers carried him off. He had remained at his post in Uganda throughout the horrible dangers of the year of persecution, as well as the years of revolution and turmoil which followed. Joined by several other White Fathers and aided later by Bishop Livinhac, he had seen an immense growth in the number of Catholic converts, building of outlying mission stations, and many small churches and schools.

He never returned to his native France, nor took a leave of absence, but remained fourteen years with his beloved Africans, giving them every ounce of his strength and life.

When it became apparent, on the morning of May 12th, 1890, that the fever was winning the battle for his life, Father Lourdel asked to be taken from his bed and laid on ashes on the ground, just as had Saint Francis of Assisi centuries before.

Mass was said by one of the White Fathers in the confines of the small grass hut where lay the dying priest who had given his life in the service of His Master. Having taken Communion, and been anointed in the last rites, Father Lourdel asked that the African Christians who were crowding outside be allowed in. They stood weeping about him and asked for a last blessing which he gave to each, weak as he was.

A great smile came over his face when he opened his eyes and saw, standing in the doorway, King Mwanga, whom he had known and taught as a young prince of sixteen. At that moment he breathed his last, and closed his eyes in death. Mwanga was overcome with grief, but it was too late. Father Lourdel had passed on to his reward.

Fever, being no respecter of men, also struck Alexander Mackay in 1890 and in only four days, on February 8th, the Scottish engineer who, for fourteen years had been the mainstay of the Victoria Nyanza Mission lay dead. He was the ninth man of the Church Mission Society to give his life for the Christianization of central Africa.

Bishops were not spared either. The second bishop consecrated by the Church of England for missionary service in Eastern Equatorial Africa was the Right

Reverend Henry Perrot Parker. He arrived in 1887 at Usambira at the south end of the lake. There Mackay, who had been exiled from Uganda and was continuing his work of translating the Gospel according to Saint John, was working on a new steam-driven mission ship for the lake. Bishop Parker had only time to meet his fellow missionaries and view some of the fine work they were doing, when he came down with ague and malaria and was dead the same night, March 25th, 1887.

In a short time the little plot of consecrated ground at Usambira was filled with the remains of many fine young men from Oxford and Cambridge, the best that England had to offer, all dead of fever or accidents in far off Lake Victoria. But in spite of the high death rate of their missionaries, the Church Mission Society received even more offers from dedicated Christians who were willing to give their lives in the service of Christ.

The White Fathers also had large numbers come to them and offer their vocations in the service of central Africa. Soon there were sixteen priests and brothers working in Uganda, and naturally the number of baptisms increased greatly. But let us go back to examine more closely the events that followed more immediately upon the holocaust at Namugongo.

Although the Christianization of Uganda continued at a steady rate, the years immediately after the martyrdom of so many at Namugongo were politically years of stress and confusion.

The first year after the holocaust, Christians continued to be persecuted and most remained in hiding. If they came to the missions, it was at night and in secret. The last of the subsequently canonized

Catholic martyrs to be killed was John Mary Muzeyi. He had been confirmed by Bishop Livinhac on June 6th, 1886, and then had gone into hiding. Muzeyi had been a prominent member of the court under both Mutesa and Mwanga and was in his early thirties. Six months after the persecution, Mwanga sought to trap this Catholic who redeemed slaves and snatched Christians right out of the hands of the raiders.

He announced that all pages who had served his father, Mutesa, would be given commissions in the king's guard and a plot of land. Muzeyi, tired of hiding, returned to the palace ready to make his peace with the king. The prime minister seized him, cut off his head, and fed his remains to the crocodiles.

Then set in a period of peace during which Mwanga seemed partial to the French missionaries. He exiled the English group, who drew back to their mission at the south of the lake in Usambiro. There they received a letter from their Anglican followers left behind in Uganda, "We are hunted, and burned in the fire, and beheaded, and called 'sorcerers' for the name of Jesus, our Lord.

"We hope indeed that in a short time other teachers will come to teach. And do you, our Father, pray that we may not in the least degree give up the word of Jêsus Christ, but do you pray for us that the Lord may help us."

The authors of this letter were two baptized converts, Henry Duta and Zacharia Kizito, both under sentence of death. They were never apprehended, and survived to become leaders of the diocese of Uganda. Both were included in the first group of African priests to be ordained by the third Anglican bishop of Uganda, Alfred R. Tucker.

The hope of these devout men was soon realized.

The persecution eventually came to an end. The Church Mission Society sent a new group of enthusiastic priests to Uganda whom they assisted greatly, working as interpreters and in translating the services and Bible. Among them was a layman, George Pilkington, who spent six years translating the entire Bible into Luganda.

Mwanga had failed his people in many ways, and in 1887 a new king, Kiwewa, took over in a bloodless revolution. Mwanga was exiled to the Seese Islands. Kiwewa, himself a Mohammedan, appointed a Roman Catholic as his chancellor, and an Anglican as his assistant, the same Apollo Kagwa who had been cruelly beaten by Mwanga the day the martyrs were sentenced to death in 1886.

Numbers of Christians emerged from hiding at last and swarmed about the two mission stations like bees. The Book of Common Prayer and much of the Bible had been rendered into Luganda and printed by the thousands. They were immediately in great demand, but the missionaries required that the Ugandans pay for all books in kind, with cowrie shells, the mode of exchange there, or in bananas and chickens. The congregation rose to as many as three hundred at the mission station.

The Roman Catholics had sent for 15,000 medals of the Virgin Mary which their catechumens proudly wore as proof of their allegiance to Christianity. These also were very popular, and helped bring many into the church.

Although there was some animosity between the two missionary groups working side by side in Uganda, one story points up their co-operation in times of difficulty.

Kiwewa, the new king, was a mere puppet in the

hands of the Mohammedans, and they soon started a second revolution. The Moslems and pagans felt that too much power had been invested in the hands of the adherents of Christianity, and determined to oust them and their missionaries from the country.

The Catholic *Katakiro* and the Anglican *Mukwenda* escaped, but the fine admiral, Magunda Isaya Kijambu, was killed in battle. The two Anglican priests then in Uganda's capital were busy dressing the wounds of the men who had fled to the mission, when they were called to come to Mwanga, the deposed monarch, by his terrified messengers.

The Anglican missionaries found him cowering in a filthy, rat-infested shelter together with the captive White Fathers, all of them guarded by rebel soldiers.

That night the Mohammedan faction raided the Anglican mission and stole all their medicines and provisions. They tore up books and smashed all the windows and furnishings, and ripped the doors off their hinges.

The next day, all the English and French missionaries, along with their ransomed slaves, orphans and the deposed monarch were hustled aboard the Anglicans' ship, *Eleanor*, and told "Let no man come to Uganda for two years. We do not want to see a white man until we have converted the whole of Buganda to the Mohammedan faith."

The two groups of missionaries then set sail across the lake.

The White Fathers had been able to save a little bit of food and some cloth for exchange. They were dependent upon the Englishmen for transit across the lake, while the latter depended on them for food.

All would have been well except for a hippopotamus which stove in the side of the boat. It promptly began

118

to sink. Bishop Livinhac, Father Lourdel and the crew swam to a nearby island, while the rest of the party clung to the barely floating ship. A native of the island went out in his canoe to bring the remaining passengers to shore, as well as some of the provisions.

Then one of the missionaries found a way to pull the *Eleanor* to shore. Later, with all working together, each contributing tools and parts, the huge hole was mended and the ecumenical party continued on its way to exile. Thirty-three people spent seventeen days paddling this unseaworthy wreck across Lake Victoria until they reached the Catholic mission at Ukumbi where all were sheltered and cared for.

Mwanga was in exile for over a year, during which time six hundred Roman Catholics and four hundred Anglicans joined their missionary brethren in exile. Finally, Apollo Kagwa defeated the Mohammedans and got Mwanga back his throne, for which he was made chancellor.

Mwanga had spent his exile in company with the French Roman Catholic missionaries at Ukubi, during which period he made a formal profession of faith, but without submitting to baptism. Then this wily monarch, on returning to his kingdom, decided to ask the British East Africa Corporation to come to Uganda to build up and modernize his nation. In 1894, Uganda became a British protectorate. As soon as the Union Jack was hoisted over his capital, and he saw the power of the great British empire, he renounced Catholicism and decided to be a devotee of Queen Victoria's Church of England.

In 1890, Bishop Livinhac consecrated a new man to take over his work, Monseigneur Bishop Hirth, and returned to France. He took with him fourteen fine young Ugandans to be trained as cathechists, doctors and schoolmasters. Included in their edifying travels on the continent was a trip to Rome, climaxed by an audience with the Pope.

On returning from exile, Mwanga gave the hill on which had stood his palace to the White Fathers where they built a fine church, Saint Mary of Rubaga. However, the consecration of the new bishop in 1890 took place at Notre Dame De Kamogo at the Ukumbi mission at the south of the lake. This first consecration of a bishop in Africa had to be rather makeshift in absence of the usual costly ornaments of a European cathedral.

Bishop Livinhac's staff managed to scrounge together a gold ring, some worn sandals and a makeshift mitre, and to cut out a tunic and dalmatic from some red cotton cloth they had brought to sell to the native women. With these poor accoutrements Bishop Hirth was consecrated head of the Church in Victoria Nyanza.

During the same period, the Anglican Ugandan chiefs were busy building a large church at Mengo, eighty feet long and twenty feet wide, which was consecrated on Trinity Sunday, 1890. The Anglicans also had a new bishop, the Right Reverend Alfred R. Tucker, previously consecrated third bishop of East Equatorial Africa at Lambeth Palace. He was the first English bishop thus consecrated to arrive at his diocesan seat of Uganda; both of his predecessors having lost their lives on the way.

The new large reed and thatch church was thronged daily by worshipers and the bishop learned that three hundred converts had recently been baptized. The members of the native church council, started by Alexander Mackay years before during the persecution, were now mostly responsible for arranging for the instruction of converts. There were only two Anglican priests in the Ugandan capital at that time.

Bishop Tucker at once laid the foundations for an indigenous ministry by setting apart six Ugandans as lay evangelists and later ordaining them deacons.

As soon as he returned to England, Bishop Tucker issued an appeal for at least twenty more missionaries. Seventy responded. While returning overland to Uganda with a party of eight new missionaries in 1892, Tucker discovered the headless remains of Bishop Hannington. These were easily identifiable by the missing finger of the former adventurous little boy, who had blown off the thumb of his left hand at the age of twelve.

Hannington's remains were carried to the capital in a box buried with great honor on New Year's Day, 1893 in the new enlarged cathedral at Mengo, the capital of Uganda. Present for the impressive ceremony was his now repentant murderer, King Mwanga himself.

By 1890 there were 12,000 baptized Roman Catholics in Uganda, twelve White Fathers, and a bishop. Besides the large cathedral church built on top of the hill at Rubaga, many smaller reed and grass churches had been built throughout the provinces.

Father Guillermain, head of the White Fathers' mission at Saint Mary of Rubaga, told of the usual Sunday scene at his church: "They are there from four o'clock in the morning, gathering around the reed fence which surrounds the mission premises. The crowd increases from hour to hour. By eight o'clock there are nearly three thousand people assembled. I advance into their midst. At the sight of the 'Father' they make a rush towards the gigantic tree at the foot of which I am going to install myself. I reach the tree not

121

without difficulty and fall on my knees.

"There is a sudden silence. The blacks imitate me, and the voices of these three thousand men recite with me the Lord's Prayer and the Hail Mary. With all the strength of my lungs I recite, sentence by sentence, a chapter of the catechism, which I do my best to explain."

Across the valley at the Anglican hill, a new church was being constructed which was finished in July, 1892. It was about a hundred feet long and made of bamboo reeds sewn together, the grass thatched roof being supported by a forest of pillars made of tree trunks standing every six feet apart. Some of the trees were brought from a week's journey away. On the day of the opening, an offering of one cowrie shell per person was taken by which means it was discovered that 3,731 natives had filled the church.

Such phenomenal growth of Christianity in a country so inaccessible and so recently pagan could only be laid to the glorious example of the many Roman Catholic and Anglican martyrs who had given their lives for Christ but a few years earlier.

The site of Namugongo began to be a cherished place of pilgrimage. Every June 3rd, the anniversary of the deaths of the martyrs, crowds came to commemorate the event with prayers and services. A brick chapel was built at Namugongo in 1926, on the exact spot where Charles Lwanga was slowly burned to death.

At the intercession of the martyrs many miraculous cures were made, and many souls brought to Christ. Cardinal Lavigerie, founder of the White Fathers and Sisters, was the primary force behind the preservation of all available evidence and historical data about the martyrs. Being in a position of great eminence, as the order had grown to large proportions, he and Bishop Livinhac and other influential White Fathers, cognizant of the tremendous power of the martyrs for good, decided to instigate proceedings for their beatification.

Usually, this is a matter that takes many years, and not something which can come to pass quickly. Witnesses, who had been executioners, or among those released on that fateful day, were now brought forth out of anonymity, and asked to contribute from their memory of the event anything which could be used towards the beatification.

The seven men still living, among them Denis Kamyuka and Simeon Sebuta, two of the three boys released just as the fires were lit, and Abdal Aziz Bulliwada, a Mohammedan mistakenly condemned with the Christians, gave their testimony which was carefully examined for authenticity. Then in 1913, the testimonies of twenty witnesses was heard and sworn to in Uganda and taken to Rome for the *Procesus Apostolicus*. This amounted to 525 pages when translated into French, and is retained in Rome in the archives of the Sacred Congregation of Rites.

Thirty-four years passed between the death of the martyrs and the official beatification, declaring them blessed and worthy of veneration in their native land. This took place on June 6th, 1920, at Saint Peter's Basilica in Rome. In the presence of the would-be martyr, Denis Kamyuka, and Father Girault, who had baptized two of the saints—Mathias Kalemba and Luke Banabakintu—Pope Benedict XV made the official pronouncement.

As the names of the twenty-two men who had suffered for Christ were called out, among them Kizito, tears rolled down the face of Denis Kamyuka, now an old man, as he recalled the words of the little martyr boy, "Do not cry. We shall meet in heaven."

Although there is no provision for canonization or beatification of martyrs in the Church of England, it does, however, recognize heroism as such. Schools, churches, hospitals and stained-glass windows are often dedicated to the memory of those who have lived or died heroically for Christ. Also, their names can be added to the official calendar of the Anglican communion.

Consequently, a plaque was installed in Namirembe Cathedral, the tremendous structure built of bricks handmade by native Anglican chiefs in 1906. Standing majestically on the hill donated by Mwanga, the great cathedral looks down upon the capital city of Kampala.

The plaque was erected in 1927 in honor of the Anglican martyrs who died rather than renounce their faith and it reads:

TO THE HONOURED MEMORY
OF THE MARTYRS
WHO LAID DOWN THEIR LIVES
FOR THE SAKE OF CHRIST
UGANDA 1885-1886

CHAPTER ELEVEN

HONORED BY ALL

When Christianity came to Uganda it brought in its wake all the aspects of civilization. Roads were built, railroads constructed, dams erected. Great numbers of missionaries and British bureaucrats brought schools, hospitals, reduction in mortality, more hygiene, scientific cultivation, industry, and, greatest of all, an end to slavery. Under the folds of the red, white, and blue Union Jack came an end to bloody battles between petty chiefs and their war-oriented followers. Peace came at last to Uganda.

In one final revolution, Mwanga was deposed and sent into exile in the Seychelles Islands where he died at the age of thirty-four, unbaptized by either Catholics or Anglicans.

The first king of Uganda to become a full-fledged Christian was Daudi Chwa, the last son of Mwanga. Born in 1896, he ascended the throne at the tender age of one year. His mother at the time of his birth had been studying to become a member of the Church of England. They both were baptized together at the Anglican Namirembe Cathedral soon after his birth.

Because of his age, a queen-sister had to be appointed. Chosen for this position was a first cousin of Mwanga, Yunia Kamwanda, already a member of the Anglican communion. Three other regents were chosen to administer the government in the name of the infant king. These were the Anglican *Katakiro*, Sir Apollo Kagwa, and the Roman Catholic *Katakiro*, Mugania, and Zakaria, the *Kangao*.

Heretofore, Roman Catholic missionaries had worked in certain provinces, the Anglicans in others, neither being permitted to infringe on the other's territory.

With the coming of the British consul and his troops, and the enthronement of the new king, all of this was done away with, and both Catholics and Anglicans were free to teach and evangelize anywhere.

The preaching of the gospel went on more vigorously than ever, while the peace and security of the country made it possible to carry the message to any part of Uganda. Grass and reed churches grew up overnight in even the most remote locality. Native clergy were ordained in both denominations and carried the message of Christ to every corner of this beautiful country of lakes and hills.

The first part of the twentieth century saw almost a complete takeover of Africa by the colonial-minded nations of Europe. The Congo came under the protection of Belgium, Equatorial Africa as well as North and West Africa and even a strip of Somaliland on the East Coast came under the protection of the French. Germany had her share in South Africa and

Tanganyika. The Italians took over Eritrea and part of Somali, while the United States even got in her bit in Liberia, where the rulers were the great American rubber companies.

The only country left to Africans was the mountain empire of Ethiopia, which had resisted invasion by Africans and Europeans for thousands of years.

With Africa parceled out to so many great nations, she could not help but be exploited and her millions of uneducated natives victimized by huge corporations and wealthy white landowners.

True, these paternal owners brought education, clinics, and modern marvels of Europe to their semi-slaves. On the other hand, the huge wealth extracted from the cultivation of cotton, coffee, tobacco, and livestock gave tremendous rewards to their white owners, while the native laborers continued merely to subsist.

But the colonialism of Europe and America bore in itself the seeds of its own destruction. As native Africans reached ever higher levels of learning and were ready for university training, they began to travel to Oxford, Columbia, The Sorbonne, the University of Moscow, etc., and, returning with the white man's skills and talents, they quite naturally wanted to run their own lives and countries.

Also, even with roads and cars and trains, travel in Africa before the advent of the airplane was slow and uncomfortable. Not many visitors went there for pleasure or even for business, if it could be avoided. Missionaries, diplomats and millionaire hunters made the arduous, month-long trip, but it was always with qualms about danger, disease and discomforts.

But all of this changed suddenly and dramatically in the period following the Second World War. Air transportation changed the face of Africa. Any part of the former dark and mysterious continent could be reached in a matter of hours. Mammoth airports grew up overnight with modern hotels not far away. European and American businessmen flew to Africa and saw her as a new frontier. They rushed to start lucrative enterprises. On those same airplanes, Africans flew off to Europe and America for education and business.

And Africans had their eyes opened. Everywhere were democratic sovereign nations. Everyone, white and colored, had cars, TVs, clean, smart clothes, access to schools, universities and government posts. Why should not Africans have these things, too? No wonder it had been called The Dark Continent. They had been kept in the "dark" about the fulness of life available to anyone who demanded it and worked for it.

Eventually the many protectorate countries of Africa demanded their freedom. With some it came easily and uneventfully, such as those prepared for it by the British over many decades. With others, it came in horror and bloodshed and gory uprisings as in the Belgian Congo. But it came.

Nation after African nation gained independence, then demanded a voice in the United Nations and took its place in the forum of the world. Africans, with their freshly printed degrees took over positions in the hospitals, national universities and governments of their countries.

Yet the black man still had many conflicts to face. It was still a white man's world. By 1950 there were twenty-seven million Catholics in Africa, two million of them in Uganda. But all the saints they venerated had white faces, every prayer book and missal spoke of the white men who had lived with Jesus, and died for Him.

What about the black man? Had his sacrifices and martyrdoms no validity in the sight of God?

Realizing the need for an answer to this very poignant question, Pope Pius XII in 1950 named Charles Lwanga, Patron of Catholic Action in Africa. Soon afterwards, over one hundred Catholic bishops of Africa petitioned the pope for speedy canonization of their twenty-two illustrious martyrs who had been beatified in 1922. Archbishop Joseph Kiwanuka was the first Negro bishop of the African continent and a descendant of one of the martyrs. He, along with the three other African bishops in Uganda, emphasized this need again and again to the pontiff.

"What the church needs today," said Cardinal Rugambwa, the first African of that rank, "are African saints who will prove by their lives that holiness is meant for black as well as white people."

The beloved Pope John the XXIII was most happy to concur, and diligently pressed the usually slow working Curia to get on with the job. He was glad to prove once more the interracial and supraracial character of the Catholic church, which he outlined so vigorously in his encyclical *Pacem in Terris*.

But this great man, although he instigated the proceedings, did not live to see them come to pass. His untimely death, lamented by all communions as a tremendous loss to the Christian world, came in 1963.

One of the very first acts of his newly-crowned successor, Pope Paul VI, was to canonize the twenty-two martyrs of Uganda.

With so many honors being bestowed on the African martyrs by the Roman Catholic church, the Anglican Communion realized that some further official recognition should be given to her martyrs as well. But what? There was no precedent for singling out steadfast and heroic Christians who had been members of the Church of England, not since it had broken with the Church of Rome in the sixteenth century. True, the Book of Common Prayer used throughout the widespread forty million membership of the Anglican communion provided for many saints' days, but these were largely Christians of the apostolic period and certainly recognized no Christians after the thirteenth century.

A book was published in 1956 commemorating saints and heroes of the faith in the Anglican communion which authorized the celebration of many more saints' days with a feast and a particular collect, epistle and gospel for each.

At the 1958 General Convention of the Episcopal church held in Miami Beach, Florida, a group of men were appointed to present a new calendar for the lesser feasts and fasts and for special occasions for recommendation to the Standing Liturgical Commission of the Protestant Episcopal church in the United States of America.

This was to be used provisionally and temporarily until authorized for a new prayer book contemplated for 1972 at which time it would be voted on by the General Convention of 1971.

This new study and calendar was published in 1963 and gave very little in the way of honor for the martyrs of Uganda. It provided but one collect to be used October 29th to commemorate "James Hannington and His Companions, Bishop and Martyrs of Uganda," in the section on lesser holy days. It reads, "Almighty God, who didst call thy faithful servant, James Hannington and his companions to be witnesses and martyrs in the land of Africa, and by their labours and suffering didst raise up a people for their possession: shed forth, we beseech thee, thy Holy Spirit upon thy Church in all lands, that by the sacrifice and service of many, thy holy name may be glorified and thy blessed kingdom enlarged through Jesus Christ our Lord, who liveth and reigneth with Thee, and the Holy Spirit, ever one God, world without end. Amen."

However, more recently, the new proposed Book of Common Prayer, published in January, 1977, with the tentative approval of the General Convention of the Episcopal church, officially commemorates "The Martyrs of Uganda, 1886," on June 3rd, and "James Hannington, and his Companions, Martyrs, 1885," October 29th.

As the observance of saints' days may be traced to the practice in apostolic times of commemorating the anniversary of martyrdom at the saint's tomb, it is interesting to note that several markers and chapels have been erected by Anglicans in the countryside of Uganda to keep alive the reverence for their native martyrs.

About five and a half miles outside Kampala on the Mubende Road, there is a tall stone cross at the edge of a papyrus filled swamp, a gloomy and uninhabited spot. Here it was that the three Anglican children, under instruction at Mackay's mission, were dismembered and burned alive for their faith. On the foot of the cross are engraved in Luganda, the words, "Blessed be God in memory of the Baganda Martyrs who preferred to be persecuted and to die rather than give up their saviour. Do not fear those who kill the body, but have no means of killing the soul. Matt. 10:28. Keep faith with me to the point of death, and I will crown thee with life. Ap. 2:10."

The actual site of the burning of the thirty-one Ugandans at Namugongo is on property belonging to the Church of England. It was deeded to them by an Anglican chief who inherited it in 1900. At this hallowed spot the Anglicans gather for prayer and witness each year on the anniversary of the martyrs' deaths, June 3rd.

However, the Catholics were able to buy from this same Anglican chief the piece of land on which Charles Lwanga was cruelly and slowly burned to death. Here they built a large stone church. The altar is at the very place where stood the tree to which the martyr was tied and burned. Above this altar is a fresco representing the twenty-two martyrs. Many people come to this church in pilgrimage and, on June 3rd, as many as ten to twelve thousand gather there for the mass which is celebrated in a large outdoor arena. At the present moment the native priests in charge of this church are trying to raise enough money to build a large basilica worthy of Lwanga's heroism.

The Anglicans, although unable to canonize their martyrs, have recently honored them by installing a brilliantly beautiful three-part stained glass window in Namirembe Cathedral. Two of the windows commemorate the native Ugandans who gave their lives for Christ, while the third is dedicated to Bishop Hannington.

This mammoth cathedral, holding three to four thousand worshipers, was built in 1906 on one of the seven hills of Kampala. A missionary with an engineering background taught the natives how to make bricks as over one million were required in the construction. He also designed and made a huge machine capable of turning out three thousand bricks a day.

When word was issued by the missionaries that many laborers would be needed to build the huge new cathedral to the glory of God, great chiefs of state volunteered their services and were shortly followed by their retainers. In order to obtain the materials necessary for brick making, the chiefs went to the clay pits many miles from Kampala. They carried the huge balls of clay on their heads back to the building site, marching to the beat of drums.

Not to be outdone in Christian witness, the princesses and chieftains' wives, went in similar fashion to the forest and carried back brushwood for the brickkiln fires. Having demonstrated the dignity of labor, these leaders were shortly followed in their work by the commoners.

Instead of a bell tower, this gothic-style cathedral departs from the usual in that it announces the time of worship by means of drums, installed at the top of its tower. In addition to the magnificent cathedral, this hill given to the diocese by the late king, Mwanga, contains houses for the bishop and other clergy, the Mengo hospital, training school for nurses and midwives, primary and secondary schools and an orphanage.

Mr. Mackay's printing press had been supplanted by the cathedral's press and publications service which employs sixty people, and has an outlet store right on the premises. As early as 1901, 100,000 Bibles and books were printed and sold by the Anglicans to their converts.

Both Mr. Mackay's and Bishop Hannington's remains are buried on this hill in the cemetery adjacent to the cathedral.

Across the valley from here is the Roman Catholic cathedral. It is an ornate Italian-style structure built on the hill formerly containing the huge royal enclosure of Mutesa. Its altar is made of the wood of the tree under which Saint Mathias Kalemba spent three days of agony following his dismemberment. Strange as it may seem, this cathedral is as British as its Anglican counterpart across the valley because it is administered not by the White Fathers, but by a British Roman Catholic order, the Mill Hill Fathers.

Two chapels in Uganda are ecumenical and dedicated to the memory of all the martyrs, both Anglican and Roman Catholic. One is the chapel of the Royal College of Budo, and the other is a projected chapel to be built at Munyonyo on the exact spot where King Mwanga sentenced the Christian pages to death on May 26th, 1886. Its shape will recall the royal audience hall where the sentence was pronounced on these valiant young men and boys, and it will be dedicated to the cause of unity and encourage prayer in that direction.

CHAPTER TWELVE

SAINTS AT LAST

Eighty years is a very short time for the Catholic church to expend in authorizing the canonization of a saint. But on October 18th, 1964, it officially declared the twenty-two Roman Catholic martyrs of Uganda to be saints indeed and worthy of the veneration of Catholics throughout the world and throughout all time to come.

All the usual requirements were met. Following the beatification ceremonies in 1920, the cause was opened once again for study and evaluation by the Curia towards the final act of canonization. Pope John XXIII hoped to institute a decree reopening the cause of Charles Lwanga, the best-known of the group, who in 1950 had been made Patron of all Africa.

But within a year it became evident that the Catholics of Africa wanted more than this. Accordingly, in 1961 Pope John signed a further decree reopening the cause of all the martyrs. Their martyrdom, and the fact that they had willingly and joyfully laid down their lives for their faith, was a known fact acknowledged in their formal beatification. But for actual canonization, two authenticated miracles must be proven to the Curia.

As it turned out, this was no problem at all. In 1941, two White Sisters had been stricken with pneumonic plague while caring for a native nun dying of that always fatal disease. These two missionaries, Sister Mary Aloyse Criblet and Sister Richildis, were quickly admitted to the contagions ward of Rubaga Hospital. The doctor, L.H. Ahmed, a Moslem, and a specialist in tropical disease, testified that he treated the two sisters with a small amount of sulfa drugs administered by mouth. In the meantime, the nuns and all the faithful began to pray to the blessed martyrs of Uganda whose relics were at the same time fixed on the ailing women.

Three days later, to the amazement of all the doctors, the two were declared completely cured. This same epidemic of pneumonic plague raged throughout Africa and, in particular, Uganda during 1941. Scores of people contracted the fatal disease and, according to Dr. Ahmed, not one survived except the two White Sisters. Also, no new cases have been reported in Uganda since their recovery.

The official decree, recognizing these two cures as miraculous and as having been obtained through the intercession of the blessed martyrs of Uganda, was signed in Rome on July 15th, 1964. The following September the final steps toward canonization were taken when Pope Paul presided over three separate consistories. All took place on the morning of the twenty-sixth of September for the purpose of reviewing the entire case and obtaining the opinions of the many cardinals and prelates then in Rome for the Second Vatican Council. The results were unanimously in favor of immediate canonization, and the pope announced that the ceremony would take place October 18th, World Mission Sunday.

It dawned a beautiful, clear day. Doves fluttered about the eaves of Saint Peter's as the hundreds of prelates, gathered there for the council, filled the stands along the center aisle. Other thousands of faithful from all over Europe and Africa occupied every seat, nook and cranny of the vast nave. Included among them were two hundred native Catholics from Uganda in their colorful costumes, as well as Princess Mazzi, a daughter of Mwanga, the king who ordered the executions, and Princess Mawanda, wife of Mwanga's grandson.

The papal procession began to the boom of African drums. Preceded by a gigantic banner depicting all twenty-two martyrs, the bishops, archbishops, regular and secular clergy of Africa slowly entered the crowded basilica. The walls of the ornate renaissance basilica resounded to the strange sounds and rhythms of an African oratorio written especially for the occasion by Joseph Kyambiddwa, a forty-year-old Ugandan composer, and sung by a fifty-voice choir from Africa.

Present also for the three-and-a-half-hour service was the only surviving sister of the two nuns saved by the miracle. This was Sister Mary Aloyse Criblet who sat in a special box reserved for the most honored guests. Seated beside her was a ninety-year-old Ugandan named Augustino Kalemba.

With all the magnificent color of this rarely seen religious spectacle, Augustino sat in the dark as he had for the past seventy years. Both of his eyes were burnt out in 1892 because he refused to deny his faith in Jesus Christ. He is the only surviving confessor of the faith from a land where so many had been mutilated and killed for their religion.

From the ornate canopied throne erected in the apse before the tomb of Saint Peter, Pope Paul VI declared the official pronouncement. "In honor of the holy and undivided Trinity, for the exaltation of the Catholic faith and the growth of the Christian religion, by the authority of our Lord Jesus Christ, of the blessed Apostles Peter and Paul, and by our own, after mature deliberation, after offering many prayers to God, after having conferred with our venerable brethren, the cardinals of the Holy Roman church, and with the patriarchs and bishops present in Rome, we declare that the blessed martyrs of Uganda are saints in the name of the Father, and of the Son, and of the Holy Spirit. Amen."

Nor did the pontiff neglect to pay homage to the Anglican martyrs who also did honor to Christ in 1886. During his sermon he asked, "Who could foresee that with the great historical figures of African martyrs and confessors like Cyprian, Felicity and Perpetua and the outstanding Augustine we should one day list the beloved names of Charles Lwanga, Mathias Kalemba and their twenty companions? And we do not wish to forget the others also who, belonging to the Anglican confession, met death for the name of Christ."

Listening closely to these words that day was the Anglican archbishop of Uganda, the Right Reverend Dr. Leslie Brown who, during the week of ceremonies marking the canonization, was the guest of the White Fathers in their headquarters in Rome. He remained archbishop until 1970 when he was ousted by the new president, Milton Obote. Brown's immediate successor, Janani Luwum, would suffer worse than ouster and follow in the footsteps of the nineteenth-century martyrs who were his spiritual forefathers.

The ceremony of canonization was followed immediately by a pontifical mass. Assisting the pope, who was the chief celebrant, was the first African cardinal, Rugambwa of Tanganyika, and Monsignor Peter Waswa, vicar-general of Kampala, the diocese in which the martyrs of Namugongo died.

During the offertory of the mass, a black seminarian made a gift of turtledoves to Pope Paul, symbolizing the joy of the saints of heaven.

News of the canonization was relayed by native tom-toms from one African village to the other across the vastness of central Africa. This had been arranged in advance by African bishops of the eight dioceses of Uganda where two million Catholics now make up one-third of the population.

From one end of Christendom to the other, the story of the twenty-two heroic martyrs was told again and again in hundreds of tongues as special ceremonies marked the event all over the world.

In the United States, the home of 20 million blacks of whom 700,000 are Catholics, honor was paid to the African martyrs in most churches and cathedrals on the Sunday of their canonization.

The most colorful was that in the Shrine of the Immaculate Conception, Washington, D.C., the largest Catholic edifice in the United States. In the presence of numerous diplomats and government officials, including the Ugandan ambassador, and an overflow crowd of four thousand, the apostolic delegate, Archbishop Egidio Vagnozzi, offered a solemn pontifical mass in honor of the martyrs. The mass, for the first time in the history of the National Shrine, was offered facing the people.

Los Angeles had perhaps the person most involved with the story of the martyrs at any service in America. This was Brother Paul Buck, W.F., whose sister, Sister Richildis, W.S., was one of the nuns miraculously cured through the intercession of the martyrs.

The following day, October 19th, the Ugandan permanent mission to the United Nations celebrated the canonization with a special mass at Saint Patrick's Cathedral in New York City.

Father John Bell of the White Fathers who was director of the Martyrs of Uganda Center in Washington, delivered the sermon. In it he said, "These holy martyrs have proclaimed for us their faith in Christ. Their vision of Christianity was clear, and although their instruction in its tenets was only rudimentary, their understanding of its message was complete.

"Through their death they have proclaimed for us the triumph of God's grace which lifted their minds and hearts above the corruption and sin which surrounded them at the royal court.

"Through that death they have proclaimed for us the dignity of the human person. Their refusal to bow to the king's wishes in matters which involved their consciences heralds that true liberty which the gospel of Jesus Christ has brought to the world."

Of particular interest to the modern Catholic world is the fact that of these Ugandans canonized in the twentieth century, none were ordained. They were, without exception, laymen, many baptized only a few hours prior to their deaths. In these days of secularization, when even priests and nuns are giving up what was to have been a lifelong vocation of prayer and dedication, the church is realizing more and more that her future lies with the laity and their acceptance of the full burden of the cross of Christ.

Like Joseph Mukasa and Charles Lwanga, it is the duty of every layman to know the facts and tenets of his religion, and to take every opportunity to spread the knowledge and love of God to others.

Also, in these changing times, it is the burden and duty of all the great churches of Christendom to minimize their differences and hold out the hand of friendship and love to one another.

The impact of the simultaneous martyrdom of Protestants and Catholics was clearly seen in June of 1968. As Namugongo is situated on land owned by the Anglican church, and the Roman Catholic chapel dedicated to the martyrs of Uganda had to be built far away from the actual site of martyrdom, the two denominations had always conducted memorial services at two different locations.

But in 1968, for the first time, this great religious festival was celebrated jointly by the two formerly antagonistic denominations. Catholics and Protestants stood together by the thousands in a single service on the eighty-second anniversary of the mass execution.

The service, drawn up by the Anglican bishop of Namirembe, the Right Reverend Dunstan K. Nsubuga, took place at Namugongo on Sunday, June 2nd, the day preceding the actual martyrdom. The processional was the hymn sung by the martyrs on their way to death, "Bulijjo tutendereza," sung to the tune "Daily, Daily Sing the Praises" of the Anglicans, and "Daily, Daily Sing to Mary," a favorite of Catholics. This was followed by a prayer led by Bishop Nsubuga, then by responses and the reading of Psalm 33, "Rejoice in the Lord, O ye righteous; for it becometh well the just to be thankful."

The sermon was by the Roman Catholic bishop of Fort Portal, the Most Reverend V. McCauley. He made a strong plea for the unity initiated by the Uganda martyrs, who although of differing faiths, died together. "The ashes of Catholics and Protestants burned on this spot, were mixed and indistinguishable. Together they professed their faith in Jesus Christ. Together they died for love of Him. We who have come here today to honor the martyrs should examine our hearts in all humility," he continued, "and if we have in any way contributed to the continued division among Christians we should ask God's pardon and mercy. Never should a day go by without prayer to God that we Christians be reunited. We must seek out occasions, whenever possible, to work together with our fellow Christians in a spirit of brotherly love."

The bishop reminded his congregation that God used foreign missionaries to bring the gospel to Uganda, but when he wanted a fountain which would never run dry to water the soil of Uganda, he chose Ugandans themselves to supply it.

The holy martyrs of Uganda, by means of their frightful sufferings, brought a river of Christianity to spread throughout Africa. Now in our battered and bewildered globe, grown small through modern methods of transportation and communication, they can bring to all men and women the inspiring example of having given their lives as brothers in the flames.

EPILOGUE

The story has come full circle over the one hundred years since Christianity first came to Uganda. During that period, thousands of native Ugandans and many white bishops and ministers have sacrificed their lives for the faith. Janani Luwum, Anglican archbishop of Uganda, Rwanda, Burundi and Boga-Zaire, had probably heard since childhood about the martyrdom of his valiant predecessor, James Hannington. The terrible fate of the English prelate may well have been in the forefront of Luwum's mind as he faced much the same situation; a servant of Christ falsely accused and condemned to death by a Moslem tyrant. Since his death, his wife, Mary, and their seven children, the youngest a boy of six, have escaped to Kenya.

Today, black Christians throughout Uganda are under imminent threat of death. In equal danger are the two hundred or more foreign missionaries stationed throughout the country. All Americans have been ordered to house arrest with impending possible deportation. The State Department and President Carter are working around the clock to provide for their safety and avert a blood bath.

But, how great and glorious an example all of them have to look up to, as they take their stand for Jesus in this present holocaust. For they know that the entire Christian world loves and reveres the brave martyrs of Uganda, black and white, Protestant and Catholic, who already have suffered for their Lord.

APPENDIX I

A List of the Martyrs

I. Those who died for their faith on Thursday, June 3rd, 1886, and who were, in turn, canonized as saints of the Roman Catholic church.

Charles Lwanga, 25
Luke Banabakintu, 30
James Buzabaliawo, 25
Gyavira, 17
Ambrose Kibuka, 18
Anatole Kiriggawajjo, 20
Achilles Kiwanuka, 17
Kizito, 14
Mbaga Tuzinde, 17
Mugagga, 16
Mukasa Kiriwawanvu, 20
Adolph Mukasa Ludigo, 25
Bruno Serunkuma, 30

II. Those who died for their faith other than at Namugongo, but who were also canonized as saints of the Roman Catholic church.

Andrew Kaggwa, 30
Denis Ssebuggwawo, 16
Mathias Kalemba, 50
Pontian Ngondwe, 35
Joseph Mukasa, 25
Athanasius Bazzekuketta, 20
Noe Mawaggali, 35
John Mary Muzeyi, 35

III. Those who died with Bishop Hannington, January 31st, 1885.

Pinto, his cook
His fifty bearers who may or may not have been Christians.

IV. The three Anglican boys who were dismembered

and burned to death in 1885.

Joseph Lugalama
Mark Kakumba
Noe Sserwanga

V. Anglicans who died for their faith shortly before the holocaust at Namugongo.

Musa Mukasa, May 25th
Muddwaguma, May 27th at Mengo
Elrias Mbwa, May 27th or 29th at Mengo
David Muwanga Njigija, date unknown at Nnamanye
Omuwanga, May 31st at Mityana

VI. Anglicans martyred in the fires of Namugongo, June 3rd, 1886.

Noe Nnuwa Walukagga
Alexander Kadoko Omutebi
Frederick Kizza
Robert Munyagabyanjo
Daniel Nnakabandwa
Kiwanuka Giyaza
Mukasa Lwa Kisiga
Lwanga
Mubi
Wasswa
Kwabafu
Kifamunnyanya

In addition, many other believers, whose names are unknown to us today, gave their lives during this same period of time. Their number is perhaps over one hundred.

Who were the Catholic Martyrs of Uganda?

ST. JOSEPH MUKASA was majordomo in charge of all the pages at the royal court. His was a pacific nature—gentle, sympathetic and patient. He was remarkable in his respect for his fellow man and for those under his command, something unusual among those who exercised authority in Uganda at that time. Joseph was the main support of the young Christian community, and it was through his influence that the missionaries were eventually able to return from exile. His peaceable character did not prevent him from interceding forcefully with the king, though in vain, for the life of the Anglican Bishop Hannington whom Mwanga murdered in 1885.

St. Joseph Mukasa was beheaded on November 15, 1885, and his body burned. He was 25 or 26 years old at the time.

ST. CHARLES LWANGA entered the royal service when Mwanga came to the throne in 1884. His personality and natural gifts were such that he was immediately given a position of authority at court and placed in command of some 200 pages. His arrival was considered a God-send by Joseph Mukasa, his immediate superior at court, and the two worked together in instructing and guiding the pages and in preserving them from the solicitations of the king and his companions. Charles was baptized by Father Lourdel on the night of Joseph Mukasa's martyrdom on June 3, 1886 when he was burned alive on a slow fire. He was about 25 years of age at the time of his death.

ST. KIZITO, the youngest of the martyrs, was only 14 or 15 years old at the time of his death. His tremendous gaiety and his musical talent, as well as his excellence in such sports as swimming and wrestling, made him a favorite with everyone at court, including the king. The purity of his life was remarkable, and he had an intense desire for Baptism, constantly begging Father Lourdel to allow him to receive it. However, the priest considered him insufficiently instructed at the time. It was only at the last moment, a few hours before being sentenced to death, that he finally received it at the hands of St. Charles Lwanga. On the way to the pyre at Namugongo, he encouraged one of his companions to "say the Our Father and suffer bravely."

STS. ANATOLE KIRIGGWAJJO, ACHILLES KIWANUKA, AMBROSE KIBUKA AND MUGAGGA were royal pages. All were employed in the court of the audience hall except Mugagga, a lad of 16 or 17, who was assigned to the private section of the palace. He received religious instruction by night, since it was impossible to absent himself from the king's private quarters during the day, and was one of the five baptized by St. Charles Lwanga on the eve of their condemnation.

Ambrose and Achilles, both about 18 years old, were close relatives and inseparable companions, even in martyrdom. When the persecution broke out, Ambrose refused to hide himself in spite of his father's wishes. Achilles, once he became convinced that martyrdom was near, went to bid farewell to his pagan parents. Despite their tearful entreaties to abandon his faith, he remained steadfast.

Anatole was about 20 years old and possessed gentle ways and a mild temperament. A model of humility, he had been a favorite of both Mutesa and Mwanga, but had refused a highly advantageous position at court to avoid being exposed to the danger of sin. When people spoke to him of the great honor attached to the post, he would simply answer, "God is greater."

All four perished together in the holocaust at Namugongo.

ST. BRUNO SERUNKUMA, the guardian of the king's armory, came from a family of warriors, which accounts for his bravery as well as a sense of superiority and a tendency toward violence. He was given to loose-living, and it was only after a great struggle with his temper and his passion that he was able to break with the past. On the day when the king's wrath erupted against the Christians, Bruno gave himself up of his own accord and put himself at the head of the group of condemned men. He died in the flames of Namugongo at the age of 30.

ST. ADOLPH LUDIGO, a member of the aristocracy of Bunyoro, had been taken prisoner during a raid and set apart for service at King Mutesa's court. He often joined the Christian community which met at St. Andrew Kaggwa's house and demonstrated his humility at these times by helping the women to prepare the meals—a surprising act for a man in those times especially one of royal blood. He was 24 or 25 years old when he went to his death at Namugongo, meeting the ordeal with his usual good humor. "The great day has come," he said. "In a moment we shall see Christ."

ST. LUKE BANABAKINTU was a member of the family which provided the king with boats for his Lake

Victoria fleet. Protestant friends had taught him to recite the Our Father, and this was the first step toward the baptism which he received later in the Catholic Church. He was one of the very first Catholics in Uganda. When the persecution began, his parents wanted to hide him, but he preferred to surrender himself in the hope of saving the lives of other Christians. He died at the age of 35, burned alive on the Namugongo pyre.

ST. JAMES BUZABALIAWO was one of Andrew Kaggwa's converts. He entered the king's service as a page and later became a royal guard and a bandsman. As Andrew's chief assistant, he was often sent to give catechetical instruction to the young Prince Mwanga, over whom Andrew exercised considerable influence. This fact was later used by Mwanga, during the persecution, to have James arrested and sentenced to death. When his condemnation was pronounced, the effervescent James was undismayed. "Good-bye!" he told Mwanga, "I am going up there to pray before God for you." He was between 25 and 30 years of age when he died at Namugongo.

ST. NOAH MAWAGGALI was a pottery worker and a tanner. Like his friend, St. Mathias Kalemba, he was an untiring apostle of the Gospel, and had an attraction for apostolic poverty. As the persecution drew near, he told his equally brave sister, Matilda: "I know there is another life and for that reason I am not afraid of losing the present one." When the king's agents came to the door, looking for Christians, Noah told them calmly, "Here I am." He was speared and, still alive, bound to a tree where he was left to be finished off by the village dogs. He died on May 31, 1886, at the age of about 35.

ST. PONTIAN NGONDWE was a member of the king's bodyguard and was often entrusted with matters of considerable importance. As a pagan, he had been inclined toward hatred and vengeance; but after becoming a Christian, he showed himself an example of forgiveness toward those who wronged him. On the forced march to Namugongo, Pontian could not keep up the pace, and at Mengo he begged to be allowed to undergo his martyrdom then and there. "I have told you that I am a Christian," he said, "so kill me here." He was stabbed to death by the chief executioner on May 20, 1886. Pontian was between 35 and 40 years old when he died.

ST. DENIS SSEBUGGWAWO was a personal attendant of the king and a cousin of the prime minister. He was savagely beaten with a spear about the head, neck and chest by Mwanga for having dared to teach religion to the son of the prime minister, one of the king's favorite pages. The next morning, May 26, Denis was hacked to pieces with knives and his body left lying in the woods. He was the first of the 20 martyrs killed during the same week in the persecution of 1886. He was 16 years old.

STS. GONZAGA GONZA AND ATHANASIUS BAZZEKUKETTA were pages in the court of the audience hall. Gonzaga, the eldest (about 24), was a model of compassion for others, always ready to help them. On at least two occasions, he offered himself as hostage for a fellow page in prison so that the latter might go to the Catholic mission for instruction and, when his execution seemed imminent, to receive Holy Communion. He was speared to death on the road to Namugongo on May 27, 1886.

Athanasius was about 20 years old and in charge of the royal dressing room and the king's treasury. Serene and calm by nature, he was universally respected and loved. Mwanga especially admired his sense of justice and his loyalty. He was martyred at Kampala on May 27, on the very spot where, six months before, St. Joseph Mukasa had died.

ST. MATHIAS KALEMBA, the Mulumba (sub-chief), was the oldest of the martyrs; he was about 50 at the time of his martyrdom. Mathias was characterized by an insatiable thirst for the truth which set him about seeking the true religion of the one God first with the Moslems, then with the Anglican missionaries. Finally, after comparing Catholic teaching with that of the Protestants, he was baptized in the Catholic Church in 1882. He became an ardent apostle and, together with Sts. Noah Mawaggali and Luke Banabakintu, would gather the catechumens of his area for instruction during the absence of the missionaries. He himself brought more than 200 persons into the Church, meriting the special hatred of Mwanga's prime minister who decreed for Mathias the most cruel death of all 22 martyrs. His hands and feet were cut off and strips of flesh torn from his body and roasted before his eyes. He died on April 30, 1886, after three days of agony.

ST. ANDREW KAGGWA—village chief, conductor of the royal band, personal friend and constant hunting companion of King Mwanga, was one of the principal Christian leaders, especially during the exile of the missionaries. His house became a place of prayer and instruction for those seeking to become Catholics, and a refuge for the Christians of the court—especially the pages who often came to him for moral support and guidance. Finally condemned to death by Mwanga, but only at the persistent demand of the envious prime minister, Andrew was cut to pieces on May 26, 1886. He was about 30 years old at the time.

ST. GYAVIRA, 17 years old, was a model of purity, defending it energetically in the midst of the corrupt court. His special duty was that of messenger. He was a friend of St. Mukasa Kiriwawanvu, but one day they quarreled and Mukasa struck the younger lad with a piece of wood. As a result, he was put in prison. But on May 26, when the accused Christians were brought to the prison, Gyavira among them, the two were reunited and, shaking hands, praised God for the grace of dying together for Jesus Christ.

ST. MUKASA KIRIWAWANVU was in charge of the guests at court. He was light-hearted by nature and was, in a way, the court jester. He was still a catechumen when condemned to death and, although he may not have received Baptism by water, he was judged by God worthy of the Baptism of blood. Before dying he cried gaily to the other martyrs: "I am happy to find you. I was afraid they might leave me aside and forget me in prison." He was between 20 and 25 years old when thrown into the flames of Namugongo.

ST. MBAGA TUZINDE, a young page of 17, was the adopted son of the chief executioner and, as such, had the most to contend with in the way of temptations and entreaties to abandon his religion. During the week spent at Namugongo preparing the huge pyre, he was separated from his companions and deprived of their moral support. His relatives begged and pleaded with him during the whole time not to throw his young life away. But he remained firm, going to his death with the others on June 3. On his father's orders, he was clubbed before being thrown into the flames.

ST. JEAN-MARIE MUZEYI was the last of the 22 canonized martyrs. A wise and respected man (Muzeyi means the prudent elder), he was often consulted by those in trouble. He assisted Joseph Mukasa in teaching catechism at court and used his modest savings to redeem young slaves whom he took to the mission where they were housed and educated. During the persecution he at first went into hiding on the advice of the missionaries. But a few months later, his mind made up to give his life for Christ, he appeared openly before the king. He was beheaded on January 27, 1887, and his body thrown into a pond. He was between 30 and 35 years of age at the time.

APPENDIX III

Excerpts from the address delivered by Pope Paul VI during the canonization of the martyrs of Uganda, October 18, 1964

" *'These that are clothed in white robes, who are they? And whence have they come?'* (Apoc. 7, 13).

"This verse of Scripture comes to our mind as we add to the glorious list of the saints triumphant in heaven these 22 sons of Africa, whose outstanding merits were recognized by our predecessor of happy memory, Pope Benedict XV, when in June, 1920, he declared them blessed and permitted the faithful to honor them with private acts of veneration.

"Who are they? They are Africans first of all. By their color, race and culture they are true Africans, descended from the Bantu race and the peoples of the Upper Nile, peoples of a legendary past, encountered by the courageous Stanley and Livingstone during the last century in the course of their hazardous explorations—peoples who settled in that part of East Africa known as the Great Lakes, where the fierce equatorial climate is made tolerable only by the altitude of the highlands and by abundant seasonal rains.

"During their lifetime, their country was a British protectorate; in 1962, however, it achieved its independence, like so many other nations on the Africa continent, and is now strengthening its freedom with rapid and spectacular advances in every branch of modern technology.

"Kampala is the national capital, but the most important ecclesiastical center is Rubaga, formerly the seat of the first local apostolic vicariate, erected in 1878 and since raised to the dignity of an archdiocese with seven suffragan Sees.

"This is a field of the missionary apostolate which received English Anglicans as its first ministers, who were later joined by French-speaking Catholic missionaries, members of the Society of Missionaries of Africa, popularly known as the White Fathers, sons of the famous and valiant Cardinal Lavigerie (1825-1892), whom not only Africa but civilization itself should remember as one of the most outstanding men to be raised up by divine Providence. It was the White Fathers who introduced Catholicism into Uganda, preaching the Gospel in friendly rivalry with Anglican missionaries, and who had the good fortune —at the cost of innumerable perils and exertions— of educating for Christ these martyrs whom today we honor as our heroic brothers in the faith and invoke as our heavenly protectors.

"Yes, they are Africans, and they are martyrs. *These are they who have come out of the great tribulation,*' the quotation from the Holy Scriptures continues, *'and have washed their robes . . . in the blood of the Lamb. Therefore they are before the throne of God.*' (Apoc. 7, 14-15).

An act of highest loyalty

"The martyrdom of the saints is fraught with drama. It is something which distresses us but at the same time stirs our imagination. The injustice and violence which led to it tend to fade from human memory, while before the eyes of succeeding generations there remains ever present the shining example of a meekness which has transformed the laying down of life into a propitiatory sacrifice, an example which never loses its appeal. It is an act of the most sublime love of God, an act of the highest loyalty to Christ. It is a testimony, a message continuously handed on to the men of today and of tomorrow. Such is the true meaning of martyrdom.

"Such is the glory of the Church through the centuries. Martyrdom was held in such high honor that the Church was anxious to gather together the accounts of the 'Passions of the Martyrs' and to compile them into a Golden Book of her most illustrious children—her *martyrology*. . . .

"Now these African martyrs add to the record of the victorious, which is the martyrology, a tragic and magnificent page, truly worthy of being added to the wonderful record of ancient Africa, which we moderns, men of little faith, thought could never be repeated. . . . Who could foresee that with the great historical figures of African martyrs and confessors like Cyprian, Felicity and Perpetua and the outstanding Augustine we should one day list the beloved names of Charles Lwanga, Matthias Kalemba Mulumba and their 20 companions? And we do not wish to forget the others also who, belonging to the Anglican confession, met death for the name of Christ.

"Pass over and help us"

"These African martyrs open a new epoch—we do not want to think of persecution and of religious differences but of Christian and civil regeneration. Africa is rising free and redeemed, bathed in the blood of these martyrs, the first of a new era—God grant that they may be the last, so great and so precious is their holocaust! . . .

"In this critical time of Africa's history, their testimony becomes a crying voice for one who heeds it, a voice that seems to echo strongly the call to *'pass over and help us'* that St. Paul heard in a vision by night (Acts 16, 9). These martyrs are calling for help.

"Africa needs devoted missionaries—priests, first and foremost. Africa needs doctors, teachers, Religious Sisters and nurses—to help the young, developing-but-still-needy Catholic communities to grow in size and stature into a people, the African people of God's Church.

"Only a few days ago we received a letter, signed by several bishops of the central African countries, begging that priests, reinforcements of priests, be sent in great number and without delay, today, not tomorrow. Africa desperately needs them. Africa is opening the way to them, opening her heart; and this may be the moment of grace that could pass, never to return.

"THIS CALL FROM AFRICA WE IN TURN BROADCAST TO THE CHURCH. THE DIOCESES AND RELIGIOUS FAMILIES OF EUROPE AND AMERICA ANSWERED ROME'S APPEAL FOR LATIN AMERICA WITH PRAISEWORTHY HELP IN MEN AND HELP THAT IS STILL NEEDED. WE HOPE THAT THEY WILL BE EQUALLY ANXIOUS TO ADD TO THIS GENEROUS EFFORT, AND PROVIDE NO LESS GENEROUSLY FOR THE WELL-BEING OF CHRISTIAN AFRICA.

"New sacrifices these are, but such is the law of the Gospel become today more than ever insistent. Charity is enkindled that faith may shine forth in the world. . . ."

About the Author

Elaine Murray Stone comes about her interest in Africa quite naturally. Her father, the late Colonel H. Murray-Jacoby, was the first United States Ambassador to Ethiopia. Appointed by Herbert Hoover, he represented America at the coronation of Haile Selassie in 1930. Both of the author's parents made many trips to Africa, and wrote books and articles on their experiences. In addition they entertained many African princes, kings, presidents and diplomats in their Fifth Avenue home, most of whom Elaine was privileged to meet.

A native New Yorker, Elaine was educated at Friend's Seminary and Saint Agatha School in New York City, then finished at Ashley Hall in Charleston, South Carolina. After graduating from New York College of Music, in piano, and Trinity College, London, in organ, Elaine also did studies in composition at the Juilliard School of Music and the University of Miami. Her early career was in music; organist at many New York and Florida churches, accompanist for several ballet companies, and finally a member of ASCAP for her many piano and choral compositions. One was recently on the program at the Kennedy Center for the Performing Arts.

But in the mid-1950s, she began writing and has had a parallel career as an author, editor and journalist. She has had five books published, over one hundred feature articles in magazines such as Guideposts, Logos Journal, Christian Life, The Living Church, Florida Catholic, New Life, and has been a correspondent at Cape Canaveral since the beginning of the Space Age for Religious News Service. She was also editor of Cass, Inc., an educational cassette company.

In 1969 she was the organizing president of the Cape Canaveral Branch of the National League of American Penwomen, and has held every office in it since then. She is listed in *Who's Who of American Women*, *Who's Who in Religion* as well as *Contemporary Authors*.

Elaine's father was a Quaker, her mother an Episcopalian, so she has been influenced by both. Her education was entirely in church schools. She was baptized at the Church of the Heavenly Rest, Fifth Avenue, New York City, confirmed at the Cathedral of St. John the Divine, and married at St. Ignatius of Antioch, New York City, to her childhood sweetheart, Courtney. They have three daughters and one grandson. The eldest, Catherine, is married to a pediatrician and lives in San Antonio, Texas; they are the parents of David, age three. Pamela lives on a boat which she and her husband built across the river from Elaine's home. (See Logos Journal, June, 1976.) Victoria, the youngest, is seventeen.

The author is a communicant of Holy Trinity Episcopal Church, Melbourne, but she and her husband attend the Tabernacle Church, Melbourne. They both received the baptism of the Holy Spirit in 1973.

Mrs. Stone has written two other books on saints, both still unpublished.

BIBLIOGRAPHY

Allen, Philip M. and Segal, Aaron. *The Traveler's Africa*. New York: Hopkinson and Blake, 1973.

The Book of Common Prayer. (According to the use of the Episcopal church, proposed edition.) New York: Seabury Press, 1977.

Brown, Gordon. *Yearbook and Guide to East Africa*, 1962.

Butler's Lives of the Saints. New York: P.J. Kennedy and Sons, 1962.

The Catholic Encyclopedia. New York: McGraw Hill, 1965.

The Catholic Truth Society. *Uganda Martyrs*. England: W.F. Sutton, 1963.

Commemoration of Saints and Heroes of the Faith in the Anglican Communion. London: S.P.C.K., 1958.

Dawson, E.C. *James Hannington*. New York: Anson D.F. Randolph and Company, 1887 (from the sixth London edition).

East Africa. Edited by Linberry, William P. New York: H.W. Wilson Company, 1968.

Faupel, J.F. *African Holocaust*. New York: P.J. Kenedy and Sons, 1962 (reprint of British edition).

Fouquet, R. *Le Bucher de Namougongo*. San Quentin: J. Fontaine et Fils, 1961.

Gunther, John. *Inside Africa*. New York: Harper, 1953.

Hallett, Robin. *Africa Since 1875*. Ann Arbor: University of Michigan Press, 1974.

Higgins, John. *The Expansion of the Anglican Communion*. England: Cloister Press, 1942.

Howell, A.E. *The Fires of Namugongo*. London: Samuel Walker Ltd., 1948.

Johnson, A. *Global Odyssey*. New York: Harper and Row, 1963.

Lambert, John C. *The Romance of Missionary Heroism*. Philadelphia: Lippincott, 1906.

Ludwig, Emil. *The Nile*. New York: Viking Press, 1937.

Mackay, B. *A.M. Mackay*. New York: A.C. Armstrong and Son, 1890.

Marie-Andre du S.C., Soeur. *Uganda, Terre de Martyrs*. Tournai, Belgium: Casterman, 1964.

Meeker, Oden. *Report on Africa*. New York: Charles Scribner's Sons, 1954.

Missi. Brussels: November, 1964. A magazine format publication devoted entirely to Uganda and the martyrs of 1885-87.

Miti, James. *Unpublished memoirs*. This manuscript reposes in Makerere University in Uganda. Miti's testimony, contained in this manuscript, figured significantly in the canonization process, although Miti was an Anglican.

Moore, Clarke D. and Dunbar, Ann, editors. *Africa Yesterday and Today*. New York: Bantam, 1968.

Moorehead, Alan. *The White Nile*. New York: Harper, 1960.

Pilgrim's Guide to the Uganda Martyr's Shrines. Kampala: Bernard Murray, 1964.

Standing Liturgical Commission of the Protestant Episcopal Church in the USA. *The Lesser Feasts and Fasts*. New York: The Church Pension Fund, 1963.

Stanley, H.M. *In Darkest Africa*. (2 vols.) New York: Charles Scribner's Sons, 1890.

Stanley, H.M. *Through the Dark Continent*. (2 vols.) New York: Harper & Brothers, 1879.

Stock, Sarah G. *The Story of Uganda*. London: Church Missionary Society, 1899.

Streicher, H. *The Twenty-Two Martyrs of Uganda*. New York: Paulist Press, 1922.

Thoonen, J.P. *Black Martyrs*. London: Sheed and Ward, 1941.

Walsh, W.P. *Modern Heroes of the Mission Field*. New York: Domestic and Foreign Missionary Society, 1901.

White Fathers Magazine, vol. 11, no. 9, Washington, D.C.: December, 1964.

The White Fathers—A Century of Service. Washington, D.C.: The White Fathers, 1966 (pamphlet).